W9-ASK-786

"ADULT FITNESS"

Principles and Practice

Fred W. Kasch, Ed.D. and John L. Boyer, M.D.

The San Diego State College Fitness Program

575

Published by
NATIONAL PRESS BOOKS
850 Hansen Way
Palo Alto, California 94304

All American Productions and Publications
P.O. Box 91, Greeley, Colorado

All American Productions and Publications
P.O. Box 91, Greeley, Colorado

DEDICATED TO THE SPIRIT OF MAN
WHICH IS UPPERMOST AND TOWARD WHICH
PHYSICAL FITNESS MAKES ITS CONTRIBUTION

TABLE OF CONTENTS

LIST OF EXERCISES

FOREWORD

The striving for a healthy balance between mental and physical prowess has been an important factor in the evolution of man. The neglect of either one of these two components of total fitness in leading tribes or nations has caused great powershifts amongst the earth's population. Progressing civilization usually removes the need of a phyically well-endowed body for survival. Man of today does not require the strength, speed, endurance and physical skills which were essential in former days. However, despite all the labor-saving devices life has not become so much easier. As life supporting physiological functions tend to deteriorate in consequence of their diminished or neglected use, the new way of life with its high educational and professional demands, severe competition, great ambitions and overcommittments requires somatic adjustments which have not had sufficient time to develop adequately. Although one might expect that the human body will eventually learn to react and to respond to the many stresses of the present and future life as well as it learned to cope with the stress of hard physical work, such evolutionary change in man will take a long time. The only available chance for bridging the existing gap in adequate adaptability is the regular training of the organic power through the familiar stress of physical exercise. The extent to which this is accomplished determines the individual state of "physical fitness".

Physical fitness comes in many forms and shades. Every healthy human being has the *potential capacity* to develop and to maintain an amazingly high level of fitness. Unfortunately, this requires regular physical efforts throughout life. Therefore, it is rarely achieved by man who, in general, likes to save energy wherever possible. If you, the reader, should be one of those who adhere to the theory that every calorie expended is an unretrievable loss from a fixed amount of reserves—pass this book quickly on to a friend. Be not surprised, however, when you meet this friend again after a year's time to find him changed in looks and spirit.

Since the image of a "fit" man has changed from the heavy, broad-shouldered, muscle-bound Atlas-type figure to a more slender, quick-moving, and apparently indestructible specimen, the general resistance against physical fitness programs has ceased. Even such a formerly demonstrative nuisance as a man running around a village block in sports dress has become a quite common sight.

As there are "many ways to Rome," there are also many ways to start and continue a regular physical conditioning program. An excellent approach is offered in this book. The authors—an efficient and sucessful physician-physical educator team in the battle for better adult fitness—speak with the background of broad experiences and know-how in the medical examining room, in the physiological laboratory, on the gymnasium floor, track, playing grounds, skiing slopes or in the swimming pool. They have worked with men at all levels of fitness including the extremes of the highly trained athlete as well as the patient recovering from severe illness. Under their guidance, many people have detected for themselves that physical activity beyond the daily chores must not be disgustingly inconvenient, troublesome and tiring, but, quite the contrary, can be enjoyable, refreshing and generating an awareness of a pleasant well-being.

Just *reading* this book will not contribute much to the achievement of fitness. Once the decision and the beginning is made, however, to try new—or to renew old—experiences involving the freedom of body movements, the adherence to the suggested programs should become a habit which will bring innumerable health dividends.

Bruno Balke, M.D.

AUTHOR'S INTRODUCTION

To us physical fitness is a very personal thing. We believe in it. It has been part of our lives for many years. Perhaps our enthusiasmiasm for adult fitness has been the prime motivation in the writing of his book, for we know that the fit adult can better adapt and adjust to the stresses of a technological world. We feel we can motivate adults toward an effective fitness program. Therefore this is a "How to do it" book. We have not tried to justify fitness nor delve into more than the basic exercise physiology. There are excellent books and monographs on these subjects. This book is a primer and guide for fitness programs.

We believe that productive, creative living through fitness is an important objective in the life of modern man. We hope that this book will be of help to persons striving to attain this goal.

F. W. Kasch
J. L. Boyer
San Diego, California
Jan 1968

ACKNOWLEDGEMENTS

This book is an outgrowth of many ideas. It is the culmination of years of discussion and trial and error. Colleagues who contributed greatly and who we genuinely wish to acknowledge at this time include Dr. J. E. L. Carter, Dr. Ralph Grawunder, Dr. W. H. Phillips, and Dr. W. D. Ross. Many other professors as well as physicians have been most helpful. We are greatly indebted to Mr. Abe Friedman for photographing all of the exercises, to Mr. Bert Shankland for the testing photos, and to David Sleet for part of the bibliography; also, Mrs. Barbara Le Sage Reemelin for the exercise diagrams and to Oliver Askew, Philip Thomas, and Sue Thompson for aiding in the photography as well as their many laboratory contributions. The typing and duplicating were mainly completed by Mrs. Harriet Halley and the grammatical technicalities by Mr. Hawley Taylor. We are indebted to the hundreds of fitness participants who have graciously permitted us to evaluate them in the laboratory and to the numerous students who have worked many long and tedious hours in collecting the data. We want to also remember the contributions of our main speakers of physical fitness institutes; namely, Stan LeProtti, Dr. and Mrs. T. K. Cureton, Dr. Hans Kraus, and Dr. Samuel Fox. Also Dr. W. L. Terry, Chairman of our Division, who gives us the latitude to develop and carry out ideas. And last and perhaps most important, we wish to acknowledge the indulgence of our wives who have so graciously encouraged our work with adults.

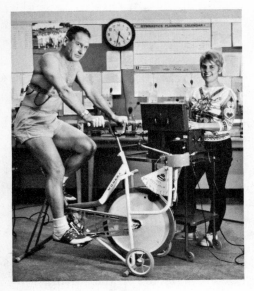

TESTING

THE COMPLETE PROGRAM OF FITNESS

JOINT READYNESS

CARDIOVASCULAR

Chapter I

DEFINITION AND PURPOSES OF ADULT FITNESS

WHAT IS PHYSICAL FITNESS?

For many years the "Charles Atlas man" was the symbol of superb physical fitness. He represented strength and power and these were felt to be the most desirable criteria of fitness. The old tests (80) to determine an individual's level of fitness were usually tests of sheer strength such as weight lifting, counting pull-ups, push-ups and sit-ups, and measuring strength with dynamometers.

Principally through the work of exercise physiologists who study and test fitness in the laboratory, the importance of strength in adult fitness has declined over the past few years. The element of endurance or stamina has emerged as the real indicator of fitness (4, 5, 9). Endurance or stamina is the ability to withstand the physical and emotional stresses of daily life and to meet the emergency demands which may occur throughout the course of one's lifetime. Therefore, in the concept of physical fitness endurance training has become more important than strength training. Continual, rhythmic-endurance exercise is the essence of fitness (30, 31, 32, 33).

Modern fitness tests measure the ability of the body to respond to work or stress. They include such factors as oxygen uptake or oxygen consumption, tests of air exchange in the lungs, the volume of the heart stroke, blood pressure and pulse rates (3, 7, 8). These are the tests that measure stamina and endurance.

Endurance training has not only become more important than strength, but also more important than skill training. Weight lifting and isometrics for strength or bowling, golf, and badminton for skill have been replaced by running, swimming, jogging and walking as the preferred fitness exercises.

WHY ADULT FITNESS

Primitive man survived largely through his physical efforts. The activity made him strong physically and emotionally. Modern man survives largely through the use of his mind and skills. Such activity contributes little to his strength, physically or emotionally. The average person today finds little physical activity convenient for him after the age of 22 years. Modern man is a victim of the soft, physically protected, overindulgent, emotionally stressful affluent society he has created (55, 56, 57).

By age 30, aging effects and sedentary living have produced various diseases and syndromes of modern life: obesity, chronic low back strain, weak abdominal muscles, high neuro-muscular tension, high pulse rates, low adrenocortical reserve, low muscle strength, low muscle and joint flexibility, low breathing capacity, shortening of ligamentous tissues, and increased susceptibility to cardiovascular diseases, principally hypertension and coronary heart disease.

The prime goals of adult fitness serve to rehabilitate and support normal physiological balance (85). They attempt to prevent or arrest the musculoskeletal and cardiovascular disorders called the hypokinetic syndromes that result from inactivity (1, 57). They restore spent physical reserves and neuromuscular and emotional tension states that are a result of the pressures of modern society. They support and train the heart muscle, the coronary circulation, and the peripheral circulation, which make for a more efficient functioning heart and vascular system.

Exercise is one of the most promising means of preventing coronary heart disease (37, 70), our nation's number one killer of middle-aged men. This "heart attack" disease accounts for a third (31.35%) of all deaths in the United States (1). Fox and Skinner (37, 38) reviewed investigations on the relationship of physical activity to cardiovascular health and disease. Their studies indicated that exercise may have more merit than any other means in the prevention of heart disease. This does not imply that other therapeutic measures are not of value and should not be used as adjuncts in the total approach toward prevention. It does indicate that lack of exercise, along with obesity, elevated blood cholesterol, cigarette smoking, emotional tension, and high blood pressure is one of the high risk factors in coronary heart disease.

THE COMPONENTS OF FITNESS

There are two components of fitness required to achieve the endurance and stamina so necessary to keep fit in our modern world.

The first component is a trained cardiovascular system. Heart and arteries that can withstand vigorous exercise can better tolerate the physical and emotional stresses of daily living throughout a lifetime (78, 98).

The second component is a trained, flexible musculoskeletal system that can provide the bone and muscle for continual, rhythmic, cardiovascular endurance exercise (53).

Training in both components is imperative for a person to be fit. This concept is basic to a fitness program.

These two components of fitness, the trained cardiovascular system and the trained musculoskeletal system, are necessary to achieve all the goals of adult fitness: progressive cardiovascular endurance, improvement in joint mobility and body mechanics (alignment, posture, balance, flexibility, and movement), and the release of musculoskeletal tensions that develop throughout the day.

THE "OVERLOAD" PRINCIPLE

Cardiovascular training in adult fitness is based upon a physiological observation called the "overload" principle (69). The "overload" principle states that when the body is regularly stimulated by a greater than normal exercise load, it responds by an increased capacity to perform physical work. In other words, the body adapts to the demands placed upon it. The more the body can adapt to the demands of exercise the better its capacity to respond to sudden stress.

FADS, FALLACIES, AND FACTS

The modern concepts of exercise, which have resulted from studies in exercise laboratories, have enabled us to understand and discard many of the fitness fads and fallacies of the past. One fallacy is that any kind of exercise is all right regardless of its intensity, duration, frequency, or regularity. Obviously, various exercises have various degrees of value. For example, one cannot improve the cardiovascular system simply by increasing the strength of the biceps (53).

A common misconception is that former athletes tend to maintain fitness even after they stop their sport. Varsity sports do not confer lasting physical fitness (13, 23, 50). Training must be on a regular lifetime basis, for inactivity causes the body to become flaccid and atrophy very quickly. Regular physical demands must be made to maintain an adequate fitness level.

Steam baths, sauna baths, mineral baths and other forms of "sweat therapy" have been advocated as fitness methods. Although they have some tranquilizing and relaxing effects, they have no true fitness value.

3

In recent years "fitness" machines have become popular. These include motor driven stationary bicycles, electrical shock devices and various forms of vibrators. They all imply that fitness can be achieved without work. This is not true (34). There is no easy way to fitness. It is attained only after many months of regular endurance exercise and it is maintained only by commitment to a regular exercise program.

Exercise fads and devices will continue for there will always be those seeking instant fitness via a gimmick. But there is no shortcut to fitness success. It can be attained in various degrees by anyone who understands the principles of fitness and applies them in a diligent and regular manner. The methods of applying these principles in an orderly and systematic way are taken up in the chapters that follow.

Chapter II

MOTIVATION FOR ADULT FITNESS

What causes some adults to begin and continue a physical fitness program while others fail? Not enough is known about human motivation to understand all the factors involved, but observations of men in an adult program over the past nine years offer some clues. These clues, together with known psychological principles, reveal some useful insights. This chapter explores these insights.

THE PROBLEM

The basic problem is that of overcoming habits of years of sedentary living and substituting habits of regular physical activity (76). For most adults this represents an immense alteration in their pattern of living. Our culture has established a way of life that daily reinforces sedentary patterns of living. Specific obstacles in our environment predispose toward this cultural inertia. These obstacles must be understood before the problem of motivation can be positively approached.

THE OBSTACLES

The inconvenience of physical activity in a culture which has not included it as an integral part of life is a great obstacle. One must find the place, the time, and the program. The resources for a good physical fitness program are not always available in a crowded urban community, so the inconvenience of finding "a place" to exercise tends to pull the adult back to his sedentary way. For the businessman under pressures, finding "the time" to exercise is difficult and frequently such an inconvenience that he never begins a fitness program at all. Many areas of our country do not have a "program" for the adult who needs guidance in fitness activities. There is no instructional source readily available to him, and he is not motivated enough to seek one out. Considerable motivation is required to oversome these inconveniences and they must be handled and discussed as part of the entire motivation program.

Discouragement is another obstacle of adult fitness activity. It may take the form of ridicule from friends and associates who joke about the "fitness kick." In addition to these external forms of discouragement, the individual subjects himself to his own criticisms

5

and excuses to avoid exercise. Against this almost universal discouragement, one must maintain continual commitment. At first, until resistance is developed through experience, one must maintain staunch determination and an absolute adherence to the program. Each concession to the forces of discouragement weakens one for further concessions. The eventual outcome is predictable.

Fear of death as a motivating force for fitness is a definte obstacle. It is a negative association and frequently fraught with tensions that are inhibitory to the fitness objective. It is best to stress the affirmative aspects of a fitness program; the vigor, the freedom of movement, the pleasure of physical effort and the relaxation and release of tensions rather than the negative, fear evoking approach (35, 36, 45). The health hazards of sedentary living, however, should be fully appreciated by one who lacks good fitness habits.

Approach—avoidance behavior is an obstacle that has been observed in a number of adults embarking on a fitness program. Typically, it motivates one to take part initially but prevents full participation in the program. There is initial enthusiasm about physical activity but as more is expected in the way of exertion and effort, attendance and performance begin to decline. Finally, participation is so erratic that it is but a token gesture to the need for fitness. One finds himself torn between his need and desire for fitness and his tendency to avoid full participation. This is frequently the result of fear of the consequences of physical exertion and is the most common obstacle in motivation. It is a common pattern of "dropouts" in adult fitness programs.

THE POSITIVE FORCES

In spite of the many negative external and internal obstacles, there are a number of positive forces that can be developed to maintain a high level of dedication to a fitness program. The first of these is the need to establish a *regular routine*. Planning such details as number of times per week, time of day, place, length of workout, and transportation are essential. Once these details are established they become a part of daily living and a habit pattern is formed. The fitness workout then becomes a routine part of one's life. Nothing short of this is likely to be successful.

Group workouts is the second most important positive factor in motivation. Commitments made as part of a group with which one identifies tend to be stronger than those made independently (29, 42). The stimulus of the group often provides the incentive to continue during periods of flagging interest (44, 72). Solitary commitment to a fitness program is more likely to occur after exposure to a group commitment. In the beginning, however, the group feeling, the group participation, the group progress and individual improvement within the group are important motivating forces.

Knowledge and meaning are important positive forces. Knowledge of results has been shown to be an effective incentive. Results from experiments, utilizing labor forces and student populations, show that in the case of those without knowledge of results dissatisfaction was significantly greater, but there was no dissatisfaction from those receiving adequate explanation. Findings such as these indicate that knowledge of results can operate as motivation through molding of feelings and attitudes regarding progress and success.

Teaching the adult to be continuously aware of how he feels before, during, and after a workout is of great value in motivation. Successful participation in adult fitness activity should provide the participant with reinforcement and confidence in his own capabilities (72). He learns to count his pulse rate at rest, at intervals during his exercise phase and in the recovery period. He thinks through what is going on inside of him as he works. He uses the second hand of his watch to help direct his pace, the duration of his work and his work intervals. He compares his performance in previous workouts with his work today. He is conscious of how much easier a given amount of work is today than it was several weeks ago. He learns to tolerate the discomfort of physical exertion and even to relish it.

The principle that the learner makes most progress when he is aware of how well he is doing is an important factor in motivation. It is the basis by which each man compares his performance from week to week in an attempt to improve it. Through the process of feedback, he feels a sense of accomplishment through visible evidence that he is achieving success in the program. The more knowledge and meaning he obtains, the better he observes his progress, the more he knows of the basics of exercise physiology, and the more motivated he remains.

In addition to whatever satisfaction individuals derive from the work itself, they seem to acquire a sense of investment in the development of skills related to their own progress. It is frequently observed that persons who expend considerable effort, i.e., invest time, energy or money to attain a goal, tend to value it more highly than persons who attain the same goal with a minimum of effort (29). The personal investment which participants have in the program, then, provides another source of continued motivation.

Progress testing is a helpful motivator. The individual enrolled in the fitness program needs to be assured and reassured that he is making progress towards some goal. Initial fitness testing of each participant at the start of his program and periodic retesting later to evaluate progress is invaluable. Participants must be kept adequately informed of their progress through frequent use of testing procedures which yield comparative results over a period of time. Discussing the results with each man and indicating areas of gain reinforce his motivation. This requires individual counseling regarding test results and fitness needs. Combined with personal guidance, counseling and encouragement, test results should provide the program with its primary motivation because individual attention is one of the most important of all motivating forces. These individual fitness conferences require only a few minutes, but often produce renewed enthusiasm and dedication.

LEADERSHIP

It is apparent that behind these positive motivating forces is effective, trained leadership. A group cannot be "turned loose" and told to exercise. In particular, the group must be carefully guided through the first phases of a fitness program. The leaders must know each member of the group so that individual help can be given when needed. Individual programs should be worked out and changed as progress occurs. There is no substitute for trained group leaders. Often the success of a fitness program depends upon the availability, the training and the personal interest of the leaders. Maintaining motivation and interest becomes the responsibility of those in charge. The stronger and more dedicated the leadership, the better the program and the more motivated the individual participant. Few individuals develop a lasting commitment to fitness without a strong foundation developed by leaders in the early stages of their program.

It is never easy to maintain fitness motivation. It is a continuous struggle against discouraging forces from within and without. The exercise habit is formed by repetition, and by repetition only. The most important positive force to help establish this habit is group participation led and guided by dedicated, trained fitness leaders. We believe this is basic to an effective adult fitness program.

In the chapters that follow we describe the basic tenets of administration, exercise pedagogy, testing and test analysis, and exercise precautions that we incorporate over a one year period in a course of "Methods for Leaders' of Adult Fitness Programs." Although this book is not primarily a laboratory manual, we believe its contents are helpful to enable one to direct and operate a functional adult fitness program on either a group or an individual basis.

Chapter III

INITIATING AN ADULT FITNESS PROGRAM (ADMINISTRATION)

INTRODUCTION

The development of an adult fitness program may be started in many ways. The following guidelines derived from our nine years of field and laboratory experience and have been successful in practically all aspects. Undoubtedly there are other ways of accomplishing the same end.

DIRECTOR

First and most important in initiating a program of adult fitness is the selection of a director. The entire program hinges on this person. He must be completely dedicated to fitness and must reflect it through his own participation and level of physical fitness. In the beginning he should lead the exercise phase and oversee all aspects of the program including the medical, legal, financial, testing, publicity, and laboratory. He must know the participants personally and have a genuine interest in each of them, ranging from fitness to occupations. Careful selection and training of other leader —instructors will follow as the demand dictates. This too is the director's responsibility. The director must continue to be fit and spend time exercising with the groups after the program grows. His personality must be reflected by the program.

Almost all persons with a bachelors degree in physical education are *unqualified* to lead or direct adult fitness programs. They need special, additional training under qualified teachers. Only then are they ready to lead adult exercise programs. Related understandings of adults is necessary in (1) pathology (2) objectives (3) methods and testing. Little or no training in these areas exists presently in most schools of Physical Education.

NUCLEUS OF PARTICIPANTS

It is essential to develop a nucleus of men or women who are enthusiastically interested in exercise and fitness. After preliminary meetings and discussion this nucleus should exercise several times with the leader. Their genuine interest should be established be fore progressing to an established exercise group. The nucleus will then act as salesmen for the enlargement and success of the group.

The participation of a school principal or administrator, a local physician or dentist, or any other professional person, may greatly help to develop a group.

Exercise groups should be limited to 20 men per instructor.

MEDICAL ADVISORY BOARD

Because adult fitness deals with many individuals who may have sub-clinical disease, it is imperative to establish a medical advisory committee. This committee will add authenticity to the project and can be of considerable help in medical-legal aspects. It should be their function to develop a code of operation. This might include:

(1) Appropriate tests and training stress
(2) Training of activity personnel for emergencies
(3) Safety devices for emergency use
(4) Acceptance of applicants
(5) Referrals to participant's physician
(6) Laboratory procedures and cleanliness

One or more physicians should be actively engaged in the leadership exercise phase of the program. He can be of great service in advising the instructor and the participants.

FACILITIES AND EQUIPMENT

Space is a necessity, whereas equipment is seldom needed for an exercise program for adults. A padded floor is preferred for executing the "preparatory" phase which utilizes many floor exercises and calisthenics. Each man needs approximately 100-120 square feet of floor space. Forty men utilize a gymnasium 90 x 55 feet. Individual mats or small pads are adequate for calisthenic-warm up exercises. An indoor or outdoor running area or track is essential for the cardiovascular phase of adult fitness. An outdoor grass field with a one-quarter to half mile or larger perimeter is ideal in comfortable climates. The usual YMCA indoor track is adequate in cold climates or a large basketball area may be substituted. Actually a 90 x 50 foot gym can suffice. It is important to have one area of known distance for measuring the ability to run for sustained periods of time such as 15 minutes.

Supplementary equipment may include stall bars, horizontal and parallel bars, horizontal ladder, and adjustable gymnastics rings.

Aids or supplementary equipment for producing cardiovascular work include: stationary bicycle, rowing machine, stepping benches, and skipping ropes. A tape recorder or piano are helpful if music is to be included in the calisthenic warm up phase.

A laboratory for tests and measurements is a great help, but not essential. The gymnasium or training facility can be utilized for the necessary testing. However, in our experience the laboratory has proven to be extremely helpful in placement of subjects into training schedules and as a motivating factor. It can start in a small fashion and gradually increase in size and potential. We believe it is impossible to gather too much data.

MEDICAL EXAMINATION

Each participant is required to have a medical examination from his own physician which clearly states his readiness for an exercise regimen. A one page form is recommended which clearly outlines the intent of the exercise program. It should be quick and easy for the physician to complete, yet adequate for the needs of the examiner.

This examination record should be reviewed by the adult fitness director and associated physician and either accepted or rejected in accordance with their findings. If necessary the medical advisory board can aid in the decision. Each prospective participant should be classified in accordance with the medical findings and re-classified later after the initial fitness testing has been completed. Reclassification continues throughout the attendance of each participant in the program. See Appendix A for medical examination form, 17A.

Medical examinations should be repeated annually or more often, partly or completely, particularly if any illness intervenes.

FEES AND BUDGET

Any program worth its salt is worth the cost. A fee should be charged at regular intervals. The fee should be adequate for the budgetary items, including: instruction, administration, laboratory fees, rent and indirect costs, publication, and publicity. Therefore, fees are essential as a motivating device as well as for solvency. Programs of adult fitness can pay their way and certainly pay the participants many dividends in health and functional efficiency.

PUBLICITY

The newspaper is one of the main means of publicizing a program. Brochures explaining the program with application blanks are of very limited value in obtaining early applicants. Television is an excellent medium and radio is of considerable help. The best publicity is satisfied customers who sell the program by word of mouth. Physician's referrals are also an excellent source of recruitment.

Feature newspaper articles with photos have been of inestimable help to us at San Diego State. Care should be given to correct reporting for publicity purposes. Often erroneous quotations and materials give misleading information to the public.

WHEN TO EXERCISE

The time of day to exercise varies with the individual involved, availability of facilities, and similar factors. Some people do well in the early morning. We prefer the early evening at approximately 5 P.M. as this is therapeutically a good time to release the tensions of the day. Second choice is at the noon hour in order to break up the tensions of the day.

An accumulation of tensions occurs in practically all occupations in modern society. Exercise is one valuable means of "burning off" the stimulus of nervous stress. To free a man from the days strain is valuable to his well-being. We believe that this evening relief is ideal for the man in today's complex society.

HOW OFTEN MUST ONE EXERCISE

Theoretically we should exercise daily for one hour. Actually three times per week is probably adequate while twice a week is an absolute minimum. Less than this may even be deleterious and dangerous and one might better continue in his old habits. Four to five times each week is ideal and should be striven for by most men. Those needing fitness the most should exercise most often because this permits the body to change and adapt. The slow change over many years to unfitness needs many months for adaptation and fitness to re-occur. The process cannot be hurried and the stimulus of exercise must be applied lightly but often. Three hours per week is less than 3 percent of the 112 waking hours. Nine sedentary men, exercising 3 times per week had a mean improvement in physical work capacity of 15 percent after six months. They ranged from 3-30 percent in improvement, while the six control subjects who did not exercise did not improve.

13

TABLE 3.1

IMPROVEMENT IN PHYSICAL WORK CAPACITY AFTER 6 MOS. TRAINING[53]

SUBJECT	AGE	IMPROVEMENTS %
1	47	9
2	51	26
3	41	13
4	60	3
5	43	29
6	40	3
7	46	32
8	48	7
9	50	17

Group improvement = 32.0 to 36.9 ml/min/kg in work capacity No improvement occurred in the controls, 34.1-33.9 ml/min/kg. We believe that the physical working capacity or circulatory function of sedentary Americans should increase from 10-30% within a year or two of proper training. This may be a conservative estimate.

CHANGE IN SPIRIT

From our observation physical fitness must become total fitness, or a part of one's life and philosophy. One must believe in it and change his goals or life plan. His spirit must be moved. It is this dedication to eventual higher purpose in life that guarantees continuation in any fitness program. One must not only change physically, but mentally, emotionally, socially and spiritually. Those who do not change become "drop-outs" and revert to their old unchanged ways.

Chapter IV

TESTING, EVALUATION, AND MONITORING

INTRODUCTION

Testing and evaluation play a very important role in the San Diego State Adult Fitness Program. They are the key to success with adults. Their purposes are:

1. assessment of exercise tolerance for prescription of exercise dosage, intensity, and type;
2. possible uncovering of pathology not found by private physician;
3. counseling participants;
4. to measure individual progress;
5. referral to the physician for further study;
6. for motivation and developing optimum fitness;
7. discovery of new mechanisms related to fitness, (Fox and Skinner 37).

Dosage, pathology, assurance, and levels of fitness are some of the essential questions the leader must have answered prior to prescribing exercise to the adult.

Continued testing and retesting of adults is one of the best motivators at the disposal of the exercise leader-director.

Before any physical activity for adults is given, there should be a complete review of the report of the medical examination from each subject's private physician. The program director, exercise leader, and medical consultant need to inspect this record carefully. Any precautions should be noted and allowed for in the testing phase as well as during the actual exercise. For example, hypertensive and post-infarct subjects must be noted and completely avoid strength exercises as well as any speed work in both running or calisthenics.

This chapter is divided into three main parts:
> **I. Simple, practical tests needing little equipment.**
> **II. Monitoring exercise.**
> **III. Advanced laboratory tests needing trained pesonnel and considerable equipment.**

The administration of mass methods using relatively simple tests can be quickly and easily accomplished by most physical education personnel with the aid of several well-trained students of high school or college age. Two periods of testing are more realistic than one. The first period is best devoted to the following areas: (1) questionnaire, (2) height-weight, (3) blood pressure, (4) posture, (5) balance, and (6) cardiovascular (step test). The second period would include the (7) power (vertical jump), (8) flexibility, and (9) muscular strength and endurance. Each period lasts approximately 30 minutes duration and with six assistants, can accommodate 30 men. (See Table 1A for suggested floor plan). Table 2A gives a suggested record form used at San Diego State. See Appendix A.

PART I—SIMPLE PRACTICAL TESTS

Initial Tests: The following tests have proven practical and helpful in early assessment of adults prior to starting an exercise regimen.

Cardiovascular

1. THE STEP TEST, Kasch Pulse Recovery Test (48)
   The most important simple test of adults' cardiovascular function is the three minute step test, or Kasch Pulse Recovery Test. It can be performed by almost all age groups and both sexes. Only the infirm or extremely unfit would find it too strenuous. The performer should rest 5 minutes before the test and not smoke for one hour or eat for two hours prior to the test.

   Equipment:
   a. 12-inch bench 24" x 16" (padded top)
   b. Clock with sweep second hand or stop watch
   c. Stethoscope (not essential, but preferred)

   Procedure:
   a. Start stepping at 11 on clock with sweep second hand.
   b. Step 24 per minute (2 every 5 second), 72 total.
   c. Duration is 3 minutes.
   d. Stop stepping at 11 and sit down on bench (step over).
   e. Start pulse rate count at 12 on clock using radial, apical, carotid, or stethoscope method. Count every 10 seconds and record for one minute.
   f. Total the 6 pulse counts for one minute and compare with normal standards in Table 4.1

TABLE 4.1

STANDARDS, KASCH PULSE RECOVER TEST

Classification	0-1 min PR after exercise	Mid-Aged Males Untrained. M = 115.0 (82-155) N = 66
Excellent	71-78	Mid-Aged Males, Trained. M = 102.9 (72-138) N = 26
Very Good	79-83	
Average	84-99	
Below Average	100-107	Mid-Aged Females, Untrained. M = 142.9 (120-186) N = 9
Poor	108-118	

Exercise prescription is easier if the results of the step test are known. People are quickly classified.

Many middle-aged men have pulse rate counts over 130 per minute. This is a sign of poor function and care should be taken in such individuals to have an ample and slow warm-up of 20-30 minutes and a four or five to one walk-run interval. This is, 50 seconds of walking to 10 seconds of running. There is some good evidence that many persons with 130 or greater pulse rates on the Kasch Pulse Recovery Step Test have abnormal ECG tracings during the exercise test (82).

The test operator should observe the test subject for pallor, undue fatigue, incoordination, dyspnea, and faintness. The test should be terminated if warranted. Recovery blood pressures are very helpful in determining the status of the subject immediately and several minutes post-exercise. A low pulse pressure is indicative of possible trouble. Such subjects should be kept horizontal and treated for faintness until the blood pressure returns to normal.

. BLOOD PRESSURE MEASUREMENTS

Blood pressure by auscultation is a helpful measurment in exercise prescription. The normal vessel pressure at rest is important to know, as elevation may mean pathology and thus exercise may be contra indicated. The hypertensive person often can tolerate some exercise, but it must be mild and rhythmic. Speed and power exercises should *never* be used, as well as exercises of long duration such as continuous running. Interval training is of the essence for the hypertensive subject.

The subject should be sitting in a comfortable position and quiet environment after having adequate time to relax. The cuff should be applied to the left arm with the stethoscope over the brachial artery at the elbow. Systolic or first phase pressure and 4th and 5th phases are recorded. Post exercise pressures may drop to near zero and thus 4th phase is used as diastolic pressure. Usually 5th phase is the more universally accepted diastolic pressure.

Post-exercise systolic pressures may reach 190-220 mm Hg while diastolic often drops from the resting value. The decrease in diastolic pressure is thought to be due to a vaso dilatation from the demand of the evercising muscles for blood and oxygen. A low pulse pressure after exercise is usually a sign of impending syncope.

See Table 3A for normal resting blood pressure values (Appendix A). Table 4A shows dramatic changes in blood pressure due to training.

Anthropometric measurement

Simple anthropomentric measurements such as height and weight abdominal and chest girth are helpful assessments and motivators to adults. Most people are interested in themselves. These very simple measurements are easily and quickly understood by most people. They are tangible. Loss of weight is often a prime motivator to persons joining a fitness program.

Girth measurements of the abdomen and chest should have a 4-6 inch differential in favor of the latter. This is not the usual case with most Americans. Other girths such as the thighs, hips and arms are also valuable in showing body changes.

Fat is a parasite tissue. It eats, but doesn't work. True, about 10 percent of the body weight is essential fat, but beyond that it is muscle tissue that works and gives a good return on its investment. Three to four centimeters is the maximum for fat folds

Normal body weight is seen in Table 5A. One must always be careful when interpreting such standards. Fat is the felon, no weight. Judgment is needed regarding body build and optimum body weight. de Vries (36) states that 3 percent of the meta

18

bolically active tissue is lost at each decade over age 25; thus body weight should diminish with age and not increase, as is usually the case.

A daily weight recording chart helps to keep the participants aware of their weight. Optimum weights should be predicted for each man with periodic counseling thereof. Behnke (15) states that weight loss should be gradual and include exercise and a minimum of 1800 calories per day, or muscle mass is lost with ensuing weakness.

Mayer (64) points out that many critics of exercise state that it takes 36 hours of walking or 7 hours of wood chopping to lose one pound of fat. Yet one would lose 10 lbs. per year if he walked one hour each day, or 26 lbs. if he chopped wood 30 minutes daily.

The San Diego State Adult Fitness Program of one hour (30 minutes of calisthenics and 30 minutes run-walk) three times weekly causes an 18 pound annual weight loss. Table 6A illustrates these relationships.

Posture

The body functions better when bones and joints are properly aligned. Malalignment of the body articulations occurs from disease, malnutrition, injuries, and actual misuse during sports and exercise. Structure is a result of function. As the twig is bent so groweth the tree. Many of the aches, pains, and musculo-skeletal problems of middle-age are a result of this axiom. Alignment, range of joint motion, and strength are essential to functional posture and freedom from musculo-skeletal syndromes. Don't neglect the feet, your means of locomotion.

The posture check list, Table 4.2 below, is a quick and simple method which indicates the trouble spots and evaluates each body segment. Follow-up evaluations are made to note progress and to counsel the subject. Certain exercises may be contra-indicated in some people. These should be pointed out to subjects involved.

TABLE 4.2

Posture Rating

Name _____ Referral, M.D. _____

Other _____

Standing Posture _____

  A-P, Head and Neck _____

    Kyphotic C. _____

    Lordotic _____

    Abdomen, Chest _____

    Knees _____

    Harvard A, B, C, D _____

Lateral

    Head, Neck _____

    Shoulder (high) _____

    Iliac C. (high) _____

    Ant. Sup. Spine (high) _____

    Grt. Trochanter (high) _____

    Scoliosis _____

    Adam's Pos. _____

    Legs _____

Feet

    Pronation _____

    Helbing Sign _____

    Arch _____

    Toes _____

General Data:

Performance

Many performance tests can be administered. Usually they are helpful to the exercise leader and to the subject. They are almost self-evaluators and usually good motivational devices for the sincere fitness fans.

FLEXIBILITY TESTS

1. *Trunk flexion (sit-reach)*
   a. Sitting position
   b. Knees fully extended
   c. Feet together, inner borders touching
   d. Hands and arms outstretched forward
   e. Reach toward bench maximally for 3 seconds
   f. Measure distance above or below bench edge in inches and fractions thereof
   g. Measures above are plus, below are minus

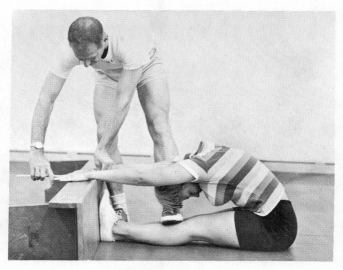

Figure 1

Normal Range
+11 to −11) Young
Mean = +3)   Men
(Ideally +1−5)

−0.49   ) Mid-Aged
(+6 to −12)) Males

It must be noted that extreme flexibility has no advantage. Plus or minus one or two inches from the mean are more normal than plus 11 inches. Flexibility holds no age preferential. It should not vary greatly from 6 to 60 years. It is lost primarily by lack of movement and an over-dosage of static positions and tensions within the environment.

2. *Trunk extension, Cureton (31)*

    a. Lie prone with partner holding buttocks and lower limbs.

    b. Rise from floor (not mat) with hands on neck firm position, hold 3 seconds.

    c. Measure from chin to floor.

Figure 2

Normal Range
2 to 21 inches   ) Young
Mean = 12 inches) Men

M = 12.71   Mid-Age
(4½-20½)   Males

3. *Shoulder lift, Cureton (31)*

    a. Lie prone on floor

    b. Arms parallel holding bar or wand in hands

    c. Chin on floor

    d. Lift wand as high as possible and hold 3 seconds

Figure 3

Figure 4

Normal Range
23 to 3 inches   ) Young
Mean = 13 inches) Men

M = 10.03   Mid-Age
(3½-19)   Males

4. *Vertical Jump (Power) Test*

This measurement may not change appreciably in most people, but often times more improvement is made in adults than in young individuals.

a. Stand facing wall with both arms extended over head.
b. Feet and chin touching wall.
c. Mark height of hands.
d. Jump and reach with one hand and mark wall or jump ladder.
e. Record difference in c. and d.

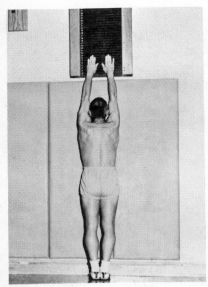

Figure 5

Figure 6

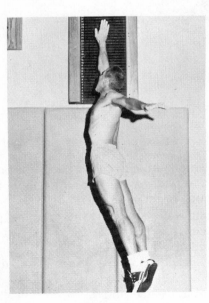

Figure 7

24

MUSCULAR STRENGTH AND ENDURANCE TESTS
Three easy, simple tests are push-ups, sit-ups, and chins (pull-ups). Each is performed to maximum, but caution should be observed, particularly in chins. These measurements should *never* be made initially, but rather after a few weeks of careful training.

1. *Push-ups* are performed with an exhale at the top. The chest should return to within 1 inch of the floor.

Figure 8

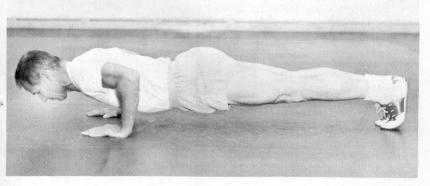

Figure 9   **Mid-Aged Males**   M = 16.5 (3-31)

2. *Sit-ups* are done with the heels 6 inches from the buttocks and held by a partner. The hands are behind the head with fingers interlocked.

Figure 10

Figure 11

Mid-Aged Males
M = 29.6
(12-100*)

26

3. *Chinning (pull-ups)* are done with regular or front grip on a horizontal bar. The pull-up is made to 1" above the chin and exhale. Lower and inhale. Normal for Mid-age adults is 5.14 (0-12)

Figure 12   **Figure 13**

4. *Mile run* is performed several months after training has commenced and the subject is in good physical condition. It must be done after 20-30 minutes of adequate warm-up on a measured distance. Running should be at one steady pace throughout the run. NEVER SPRINT THE LAST POR-TION (it will gain only 3-5 second and may be disastrous). Set a slow pace and run each quarter mile at a predetermined rate. Lap time should be called by the timer to help pace. Large groups can run at one time with each man remember-ing his time. Teach pace by using 440 yd. run and later with slow mile time using leaders with each group. Use care and judgment. The 15 min. run is better and safer.

5. *Fifteen (15) minute run (for distance)* has been advocated by Dr. Bruno Balke (12), a physician and renowned fitness expert. The subject runs at a steady rate over a measured course for a total of 15 minutes. Thus, all subjects start and stop running simultaneously and end at different positions on the track or marked course. Each man must remember his laps and calculate his distance. Table 7A in Appendix A gives the values. Six sedentary men who trained for one year averaged 198 meters/min (183-211). This is a simple method of calculating Vo₂ and thus, circulatory function. Average is 150 meters per minute and Vo₂ of 37 ml/min/kg.

Table 8A gives the levels for some American college students, while 9A gives laps and Vo₂.

6. *Running for minutes 2, 3, 4, 6, 8, and 10.* Early in the training session, slow running for specified amounts of time may be helpful in evaluating cardiovascular fitness. After the initial three months of 30 seconds alternate run-walk, the exercise tolerance improves (see chapter on Program, 1-3 mos.). At such time, a continuous 2 min. run, with recovery Heart Rate may be used to observe improvement in circulatory func-function. Later, a 3 min. run may be tried and again, 4 minutes until a maximum of 8 or 10 minutes is completed. Heart rates must be counted to avoid over-stress. They should be below 150, depending upon age and maximum Heart Rate. Perhaps some should be less than 120, such as in the case of some hypertensives or other cardiacs or emphysema patients. See section on monitoring which follows in this chapter.

Remember! Don't Sprint! Run Steady Pace.

PART II—MONITORING EXERCISING SUBJECTS

Monitoring begins with the original medical assessment by the physician. The Medical form is reviewed simultaneously by the exercise leader, program-laboratory director, and the medical advisor. Next, the exercise leader continually observes and assesses each man at every exercise session and as often as necessary in accordance with need. The step test data and Heart Rate during the running are also helpful adjuncts. In addition, musculo-skeletal problems are noted and flexibility and strength observed. The subject may be returned to his physician for further study if warranted.

This arrangement becomes a two-way street with information and data being passed in both directions.

Two studies of importance are cited: Astrand et al. (8) and Karvonen (47, 46), which gives us additional data for training changes and monitoring. Astrand found the HR at 40% of maximum working capacity to be 110 and at 100% to be 186. The maximum stroke volume also occurred at 40% and 110 HR, but cardiac output was not impaired up to Heart Rates of over 200 per minute.

Using this data for men, one may calculate the heart rates in percent of working capacity. This verifies the 70% working heart rate procedure for training the heart as outlined by Karvonen (47). Assuming a resting heart rate of 60, the following Table 4.3 is suggested.

TABLE 4.3

HEART RATE AND WORK LEVEL

Percent work — HR		Percent work — HR	
0	60*	60	135
10	73	70	147
20	85	80	160
30	98	90	172
40	110**	100	186***
50	123		

$$*\text{Resting} \quad HR = 60$$
$$**40\% \text{ Vo}_2 \quad = 110 \quad (\text{maximum stroke volume})$$
$$***100\% \text{ Vo}_2 \quad = 186$$

Karvonen's formula is:

$$(\text{Max HR} - \text{Resting HR}) \times 70\% + \text{Resting HR} = \text{Exercise HR}$$

$$
\begin{array}{ll}
186 & 88 \\
-\ 60 & +\ 60 \\
\hline
126 & 148 \text{ Exercise HR} \\
\times\ 70\% & \\
\hline
88.2 &
\end{array}
$$

Thus, it is suggested in order to make changes or improvement in cardiovascular function that the Exercise Heart Rate be at the 70 percent level after the initial three months training and 60% during the initial three months. Refer to Table 10A in Appendix A. This working level must be sustained over a period of several minutes and up to 15 minutes or longer. Karvonen (46) found that initial changes occurred after four weeks training in young men running for a 30 minute period four to five times per week. This method is a bit ambitious for middle-aged men and thus should be curtailed and a lesser program designed. *Time is in favor of the middle-aged man if he will permit himself to progress slowly.* Thus, he may need 6-12 months or more to make substantial gains in fitness.

Getting maximum Heart Rate may be dangerous and unnecessary. An assumed maximum HR is available by using the average from Table 4.4. Resting HR is obtained in the morning prior to arising, averaging several days rates.

TABLE 4.4

MEAN MAXIMUM HEART RATE BY AGE IN MEN

Source	31-40	41-50	51-60
Kasch, et al.	187	185	178
	(184-194)	(167-204)	(154-191)

It is recommended that the Karvonen formula be used as a monitoring method, or that the heart rate stay below 144 during the first three training months and below 150 during the third to the sixth month. After six months, the 70% working heart rate is used.

Precaution—Check the heart rate for 10 seconds after the running or other exercise phase to see if it is consistently high or low. It is better to err on the low side during early months of training. It is suggested that the lower level of the range for maximum heart rate be used, i.e., age 51-60, 154. This can be corrected to a higher rate as experience indicates.

The subject should be taught to count his or her heart rate during the first few class sessions, using palpation of one carotid pulse. The instructor should check the count for accuracy. Continual revision of the running schedule is necessary. Both the physician and instructor should be continually checking heart rates and revising the running programs accordingly.

The use of heart rate is a simple and practical method of monitoring. It permits the individual to run (and walk) at his or her own rate and distance independent of other runners. This becomes true individualizing. It is safe and better than using distance or time alone during the early phase of training. This method may be changed later, after known levels of work and Heart Rate have been established.

Experience has shown that changes can be made in soft Americans. Kasch and associates (53) exercised sedentary middle-aged American males three times per week for 60 minutes each period and found an average increase in maximum work capacity of 20% after 12 months. The first 3 months' training consisted of mostly calisthenics and "easy" intermittent running-walking. The last nine months consisted of 20-25 minutes of calisthenic warm-up and 30-35 minutes of intermittent running followed by 5 minutes of flexibility "cool-down" exercises. Table 4.5 shows the kind of gains possible by sedentary American men.

TABLE 4.5

CHANGES IN MAXIMUM Vo_2 WITH 12 MOS. TRAINING, MALES 40-60 YRS.

Group	Max Vo_2, ml/min/kg Baseline	Max Vo_2, ml/min/kg 12 mos.	% Change
Experimental (N-9)	32.0 (28.0-38.5)	38.5 (28.2-47.0)	20
Control (N-6)	33.9 (26.0-41.2)	34.1 (27.0-41.2)	0

Other changes may be seen in Table 11A, Appedix A.

These circulatory and endurance improvements are quite exceptional and unexpected in view of the extremely poor initial function. The "soft American" can usually be partially saved if he tries. The degree of this recovery is probably limited by the man's original maximal development betwen ages 20-25 years.

PART III—ADVANCED LABORATORY TESTING

Although advanced laboratory tests are complicated, expensive and time consuming, they are extremely valuable and helpful aids in Adult Fitness. They tell us many things about circulation and pulmonary function. They are not without some risk, yet it is minimal if properly conducted and monitored with an ECG (electrocardiography). A physician should be in attendance who is associated with the laboratory.

Maximal oxygen uptake, prediction of maximal oxygen uptake, pulmonary function, and anthropometry are all helpful in carefully assessing subjects for exercise prescription.

31

Maximum Oxygen Uptake

The limiting factor in prolonged work in man is oxygen. Work may be measured mechanically or indirectly by the amount of oxygen utilized. Oxygen consumption and oxygen intake are synonymous with oxygen uptake (Vo_2). To measure Vo_2, the subject must be stressed for several minutes, according to Astrand (9) and Sjostrand (91). A short test does not call on the cardiac reserve or adequately stress the cardiovascular system.

The main purpose in determining the maximum Vo_2 is to indirectly measure the circulatory capacity or function. Simonson and Enzer (90), as well as Mitchell et al. (67), state that if the lungs are intact Vo_2 measures the circulatory function. Astrand (9) states that Vo_2 may tell us more than when measuring the cardiac output. Asmussen and Nielsen (3) found cardiac output to be linear to Vo_2.

It is the circulatory function or capacity and the improvement thereof that we are attempting to accomplish with cardiovascular-respiratory exercise, i.e., running, swimming, cycling. Standards of Vo_2 or circulatory capacity are available in Table 7A (Balke), Table 12A (Astrand), and Table 13 A (Robinson).
Per Olaf Astrand (11) states that it is the improvement in Vo_2 and maintenance of a high level which is "all important." Some individuals initially or hereditarily may have a high capacity. This may lead them to be complacent and shun exercise. It may continue to remain high, but yet it will not be of greatest value to the circulatory function and possible prevention of "coronary heart disease" unless training and improvement occur.

Three acceptable methods for exercising the subjects are available to measure maximum Vo_2: (1) step, (2) treadmill, and (3) bicycle ergometer. Each has certain advantages and drawbacks. All use the same basic principle—maximally stress the cardio-respiratory system.

There are two methods of measuring Vo_2. We shall discuss what is generally considered the better of the two, the "open system" or Douglas Bag Method as described by Consolazio (27). In this system, the subject is stressed to maximum aerobic or circulatory capacity for 1-2 minutes after gradually increasing the work load for 5-10 minutes. A warm-up period of 5-10 minutes has preceded this period with a 10-minute rest intervening. The exhaled air is collected at 30 or 60 second intervals in lightweight meteorological balloons with large adapted necks. Three air samples are taken from each bag and analyzed by the method of Scholander (88) for O_2, CO_2, and N_2. The contents of the bag are measured with a wet-test gasmeter (American Meter Co., AL19) at a constant flow rate of 40 L/minutes and corrected to standard temperature and pressure dry (STPD). The "True O_2," or percent of O_2 extracted from the lungs, is obtained from a line chart (Consolazio). Knowing the volume of air and the percent of O_2 extracted, the calculation is simple:

$$\text{Ventilation in } L(STPD) \times \text{True } O_2 = O_2 \text{ Uptake } (Vo_2)$$

To compare the Vo_2 or O_2 uptake, the result must be divided by kilograms of body weight of the subject. Thus, the final result is calculated as ml/min/kg. It may be that only the kg of lean body mass (LBM) should be used as a more accurate figure of working tissue. A high result indicates a greater capacity of the cardio-respiratory system for work. Subjects with low Vo_2 must be given a lesser exercise prescription than those with greater capacity. One of the main objectives of Adult Fitness is to increase the Vo_2 with exercise. Knowing the maximum Vo_2, Heart Rate, blood pressure, pulmonary ventilation, ECG tracing, and thus, the exact response of the subject, we can accurately design the amount of exercise to give each man. Although 70 percent is considered the optimum level of work to improve the Vo_2, or circulatory capacity, in some cases we may use only 40 or 50 percent and others as much as 90 percent.

Table 14A gives comparisons of Vo_2 and Heart Rate for various ages and both sexes.

The reader is referred also to the works of Astrand (5), Robinson (79), Kasch, et. al. (50) and Taylor, et al. (95) for further details of techniques and levels of capacity.

THE STEP TEST

The *step test* has been used in many forms, but seldom as a device for inducing maximum work. Kasch and associates (50, 51) have used a 12-inch bench with increasing stepping rates for 6-12 minutes duration to develop maximum Vo_2. By keeping the bench low and starting with a rate of 24 per minute, the cardio-respiratory system has been maximally stressed for aerobic work and without inducing anaerobic leg fatigue, which higher stepping benches appear to do. The bench cost is nil, it is easy and safe to use, it is portable, and easily stored.

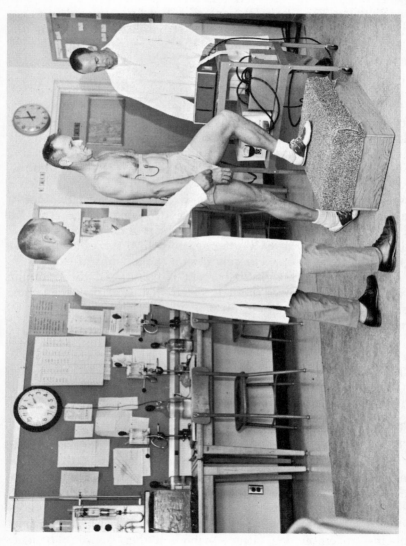

Figure 14

34

The step test technique for maximal Vo_2 follows:

1. Preliminary practice of the subject using the mouthpiece while performing the step test is given several days prior to the full test. This aids in minimizing the learning effect and indicates the heart rate and other responses of the subject. The subject is stressed to about 80% of maximum.

2. The subject is tested in the early morning in the fasting state.

3. A warm-up is given on the step bench (12") for 5-7 minutes, increasing the heart rate to 140-180 beats per minute or 80% of the maximum Heart Rate or capacity of the individual. The rest period is 10 minutes.

4. Heart rate is obtained by ECG using a V4 lead with all three electrodes on the the thoracic cage, and using a rubber strap. Two electrodes are placed one under each nipple, and the ground (right leg) electrode placed on the right back side of the thoracic cage. If an ECG is not available, a stethoscope with long tube and chest harness is substituted. The Heart Rate is counted and recorded at 10 second intervals throughout exercise and recovery. The step bench is padded, placed on a rug, and the subject steps barefooted to minimize the noise.

5. Stepping rate usually starts at 24 per minute and is increased after 2-3 minutes about 3 each minute until maximum. Maximal rates usually range between 37-60. The object is to increase rate without developing anaerobic leg fatigue which occurs with high benches.

6. Indications of maximum Vo_2 are (a) Heart Rate, (b) drop off in stepping rate and coordination, (c) blanching of skin, (d) a drop in O_2 saturation as seen with a recording ear oximeter.

7. Collection is generally during the last 3-4 minutes and is started when the Heart Rate is above 80 percent of maximum. Bags are a minimum of 30 ± 2 seconds and preferably 60 seconds (74). Meteorological ballons (49) are used for air collection.

8. Three samples are drawn from each meteorological balloon, or collection bag, and analyzed for CO_2, O_2, and N_2 according to the method of Scholander (88). The tolerance for samples is 0.05% between two different operators and machines. The "True O_2" or percent of O_2 extracted from the pulmonary circuit, is calculated or obtained from the line chart in Consolazio (27).

9. The pulmonary ventilation is measured at a steady flow rate of 40 L per minute in a wet-test gas meter and corrected for STPD using Carpenter's Tables (24).

Calculation of Vo_2 is obtained from the following formula:
Ventilation (corrected for STPD and time) $\times$ True O_2 = O_2 uptake.

For a complete review of the calculations see Consolazio (27).

THE TREADMILL TEST

The *treadmill* ($2,000-6,000) for measuring maximum Vo_2 has been used in the same manner as the step test; that is, increasing rate throughout the test. The step test correlates very high (0.95) with the treadmill method of obtaining Vo_2 and can, therefore, be interchanged for practical purposes. The cost of a treadmill is often prohibitive and thus a 12" step can be substituted at practically no cost.

Figure 15

The treadmill technique is the same as that of the "step tests" (50, 52). In addition, the treadmilll is horizontal while the rate is gradually increased to the maximum tolerance of the subject similar to the method of Robinson (79), execept that the duration is longer (6-12 min.).

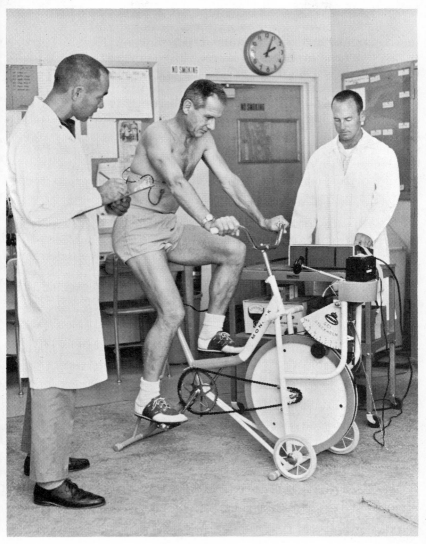

Figure 16

THE BICYCLE ERGOMETER TEST

The *bicycle ergometer* ($300-2,500) is a convenient instrument for developing maximum oxygen uptake. The amount of physical-mechanical work can be nicely measured and collection of gases is simple. Again, we use the increased rate method of inducing circulatory stress rather than the constant rate approach of Astrand (5). A revolution counter is necessary for recording the RPM and eventual determination of the kilogram meters of work (Kgm). Approximately 6 percent lower Vo_2 is found with the bike as compared with the step test. One drawback to the bike is an apparent pooling of blood in the lower extremities after the test. This has caused us much concern. The pulse pressure becomes very low and syncope (fainting) occurs in some subjects. A careful watch of the blood pressure for 10-15 minutes after cessation of exercise is recommended prior to release of the subject. Sjostrand (91) cautions on the danger of cold showers immediately following a heavy bout of exercise and recommends a 15-minute reclining recovery period.

SUB-MAXIMAL BICYCLE TEST

The Astrands (6) have devised a sub-maximal bicycle ergometer test for the prediction of work capacity or Vo_2. The subject pedals at 50 RPM at "steady state" with load increments being determined by HR between 120-170 during the 5th and 6th minutes of pedalling, the two counts having a range of 5 beats or less. Age and HR corrections are available.

Although this is a safer and less demanding test, its validity has been questioned.

The reader is also referred to the Sjostrand 170 PWC (Physical Work Capacity) test (91) as another Heart Rate test of value in assessing circulatory function.

THE ELECTROCARDIOGRAPH (ECG) IN EXERCISE

Dr. A. M. Masters reported the Master's Two Step ECG Test (60, 61, 62, 63) in 1944, which measured the ECG immediately after exercise. About 1954, exercise ECG tracings were started, although telemetering had been performed many years earlier. In 1960, La Due (58) demonstrated the exercising ECG, using direct wire connections. Since then, many workers have used his or similar methods.

The ECG tracing during exercise gives important information which is unobtainable at rest (58, 87). It has one drawback: usually only one lead can be traced. This gives limited information. Some costly ECG machines simultaneously record up to six leads. The ECG is a clinical instrument which should be interpreted only by a physician. Heart rates may be obtained without using the clinical record.

Prior to exercising patients, a standard 12 lead resting ECG should be given. If this is normal, an exercise ECG may be administered. With normal subjects there usually is no problem in giving an exercise ECG. The "hard-line" or direct wire method is very satisfactory if the chest strap is secure and a small amount of electrode paste is used with standard limb electrodes. We cut our electrodes down slightly to reduce the surface area, which in turn makes them more comfortable for the subject. The V4 chest lead is used with the second electrode being placed under the right nipple and the right leg or ground electrode is placed on the posterior right thorax. This is the method of Horvath (43). The remaining two lead wires are wrapped out of the way and attached to the posterior waist band of the subject's trunks. The instrument sensitivity is set at one-half standard to eliminate the tracing from moving off the paper.

Monitoring of Heart Rate and ECG tracing is an important part of any exercise procedure. The physician can easily see if any abnormalities occur and can terminate the test if necessary. The ECG during the maximum Vo_2 is a very helpful tool, particularly when working with middle-aged subjects.

Telemetering the ECG has not been done in our laboratory. It is a very helpful instrument in monitoring Heart Rates during training. However, it is not without technical problems, one of which is range. In the laboratory, the direct wire method is easier and cheaper and can do about everything the telemetering can do.

PULMONARY FUNCTION

Tests of pulmonary function are many and extremely complicated. They usually require a pulmonary specialist for interpretation and diagnosis. See Comroe (26) for further details. Two rather simple tests to administer which give limited information are MBC (maximum Breathing Capacity) and the TVC (Timed Vital Capacity). A 13.5 liter spirometer is used. Subjects such as the asthmatic and emphysematous can usually (but not always) be quickly detected with these two tests. These subjects have difficulty in cardio-respiratory activities and must be carefully controlled.

39

The MBC test is usually of 12 seconds (10-15) duration with continuous ventilation. The volume recorded on the Kymograph paper is multiplied by 5 to give a minute value, then by the BTPS factor, and compared to a standard such as that of Motley (71). A value of 100% is normal with a range of about ± 20%.

PREDICTION OF MBC, MOTLEY (71)

Males (adult) $= (97 - \frac{1}{2}$ age$) \times$ surface area in $M^2 = L/min.$

Females (adult) $= (86 - \frac{1}{2}$ age$) \times$ surface area in $M^2 = L/min.$

The TVC is a one exhalation measurement. The subject is asked to perform a maximum inhalation and exhale all of the air as rapidly as possible. The value on the Kymograph is recorded for 1, 2, and 3 seconds and at full expiration. The values are then corrected for BTPS (Body Temperature and Pressure Saturated). The criteria are: 75% exhalation in 1 second, 85% in 2 seconds, and 95% within 3 seconds. Comroe uses 25 ml/cm height as a norm for volume.

TABLE 4.6

BTPS FACTORS, FROM COLLINS MANUAL ON SPIROMETRY (25)

Gas Temp (C)	Factor	Gas Temp (C)	Factor
20	1.102	29	1.051
21	1.096	30	1.045
22	1.091	31	1.039
23	1.085	32	1.032
24	1.080	33	1.026
25	1.075	34	1.020
26	1.068	35	1.014
27	1.063	36	1.007
28	1.057	37	1.000

The reader is referred to Table 15A and Table 16A in Appendix A for calculations of MBC and TVC.

Chapter V

EXERCISE PRINCIPLES FOR ADULTS
(Twenty Principles for the 20th Century)

INTRODUCTION

The word "exercise" has many connotations. It is often used as a general term, whereas it has a specific meaning. Exercises for adults are different from those for youngsters. "Cardiovascular exercises" have a specific purpose; that is, the training of the heart, circulatory, and associated systems. They are of little value in stretching shortened connective tissue around a joint or muscle group. Conversely, "stretching or flexibility exercises" are of little value in cardiovascular development. Thus, specific exercises must be utilized for special purposes. Likewise, each discipline or branch of learning needs certain rules or principles to act as guidelines for action. Thus it is with the discipline of "Adult Fitness." The following principles will act as our guidelines for action.

TWENTY PRINCIPLES OUTLINED

1. Medical examination
2. No alcohol prior to exercising
3. Warm-up
4. Lateral trunk flexion prior to forward trunk flexion
5. Proper sequence of exercises
6. Exhale on each exercise repetition
7. Avoid arm support exercises
8. Tilt table effect
9. Slow and rhythmic
10. Time is in your favor
11. Interval training
12. Specific warm-up
13. Concentrate on cardiovascular
14. Individualize programs and gradually increase dosage
15. Follow trunk hyperextension with trunk flexion
16. Good Leadership
17. Avoid isometrics

18. Regularity
19. Taper-off and relax
20. Avoid over-fatigue

TWENTY PRINCIPLES DEFINED

Medical examination

As a precautionary measure and for optimal health, a medical examination should precede any newly assumed program of exercise. In certain abnormal health conditions, exercise may be contra-indicated. Only your physician can approve you for exercise and will know of any abnormal problems. Physical fitness cannot be fully achieved without freedom from correctable defects. An annual medical examination is an integral part of every physical fitness program. It is a part of the preventive medicine which is one of the aims of all *Adult Fitness Programs*. See sample form in Appendix A-17A.

It must be pointed out here that some pathological conditions are improved by therapeutic exercise and that they should be known to the medical associate and the exercise leader in order to prescribe scientifically.

No alcohol prior to exercising

Evidence is at hand which shows that a vaso constriction of the coronary arteries of the heart occurs with the intake of alcohol (97). This appears to be a potentially dangerous practice prior to exercising, for a vaso dilatation or increased opening of the coronary vessels is essential to the oxygen demand of the heart. Thus a vaso constriction is to be avoided and subjects should abstain from any alcoholic beverages for at least 4-5 hours prior to exercising and minimize it at other times.

Warm-up

This is essential prior to any exercising as it readies the joints for further action by increasing the synovial flow (fluid of joints) and by thickening the joint (collagen) tissue (94).

The body systems need *TIME* to adjust from rest to exercise conditions. Neuro-muscular coordination, reflexes, and joint readiness are preparatory to the later demands for running or other types of cardiovascular work.

Lateral Trunk Flexion

Lateral trunk flexion or trunk rotation should always precede forward flexion of the trunk. The former movements should also be initiated early in the warm-up process. The muscles of the spine and back contract eccentrically during trunk forward flexion. They are in need of relative relaxation and release of tension due to the human upright posture. By bending laterally, one spinal muscle set contracts and the other set releases or reciprocates and relaxes, (Sherrington) (28). After this relaxation of the posterior spinal muscles, forward flexion becomes easier and the muscles release their tension.

Sequence of exercises

The warm-up exercises follow a definite pattern and order. They are not haphazard. The progression of body joints should be: (1) shoulder, (2) hip and spine, (3) knee, (4) neck, and (5) ankle and foot. Although there may be no known scientific order, this sequence has proven to be satisfactory in our experience.

Exhale on each exercise repetition

Forced expiration should occur on each repetition during the contractile portion of each and every exercise to avoid breath holding and closing of the glottis. During this maneuver (Valsalva), the stroke volume and cardiac output of the heart are diminished (19, 21, 59, 66, 81, 89, 101) due to the decrease in venous return caused by an increase in intra-thoracic pressure. During exercise the body and heart in particular demand a greater amount of O_2; thus a decrease in cardiac output causes a loss of O_2 to the tissues when it is needed most. This may become dangerous, particularly in pathological cases, i.e., coronary heart disease, asthma, emphysema, or hypertension.

Prevent the occurrence of valsalva by forced expiration on each exercise during the effort or contractile stage.

Avoid arm support exercises

In the first few months of training, arm support exercises such as push-ups are to be avoided. *Arm support and hanging exercises* of a purely strength or muscular endurance variety should be minimized for adults. Astrand (10) has shown that the blood pressure (in the femoral artery) is 20-25 mm Hg greater during arm work as opposed to leg work. This in turn would lead us to believe that it may be safer to exercise the legs, particularly in middle-aged persons and ones who may have some narrowing of the coronary vessels of the heart. We have seen the value of leg as opposed to arm exercise in post-infarct (heart attack) subjects. Shortness of breath and increased stress appear in these subjects during the early weeks of training with arm work.

No explanation of this blood pressure differential is given by Astrand and his associates. We would venture to say that it may be caused in part by the apperent needed fixation of the trunk and respiratory muscles when using the arms. The partial or complete closing of the glottis (Valsalva) is also involved (18).

Tilt table effect
The use of gravity by changing the body position from vertical to horizontal and vice versa is an aid to the circulatory system. Blood flow is more easily conducted in the horizontal position without the long hydro-static pressure of the bipedal or upright posture. Thus the change from horizontal to vertical and return to horizontal is a helpful method in the rehabilitation of the cardiovascular system of the middle-aged person. It also appears to be effective in relieving muscle tension by releasing the effect of gravity.

Slow and rhythmic
Exercises should be *slow and rhythmic*. Avoid speed and the "drive-drive," "push-push" type. The latter may be for kids, but adults aren't kids.

a. Give the body time to adjust
b. Tight tissue may tear and must have time to adapt and stretch
c. Relaxation comes from rhythmic exercise, not from the "push" type
d. Give the body time to move through a full range of joint motion. This will aid in improving the cordination of body movement as well as improving joint flexibility and relaxation.

Time is in your favor
Avoid hurrying and rushing into exercise. It usually takes from 5-25 years to become unfit. Therefore, allow adequate time in years for old tissue to adapt and become pliable. Tissue will change, but you need patience. *Don't be a fool*, especially an *old fool*. You can't regain your youth, but you can almost do it. *Time* will perform the

MIRACLE. Enjoy TIME. Don't make it a chore. Adults rehabilitate at varying rates. Allow 1-4 years. *Hurrying may cause death,*
not fitness. Persevere and exercise daily. "Father Time" will eventually get you, but let him wait.

**It is better to exercise for long periods at a low intensity than to
attempt to squeeze in at a high intensity in a short time span.**

Interval training

Interval Training is the key to cardiovascular endurance. It is a
training method which uses intervals of work and semi-rest. It
permits the body to adjust or "adapt" to the work load by alternately
working and resting. It also permits the individual to increase his
(or her) tolerance for exercise over a period of time (92). Each
person, regardless of ability, can use it to work at his own level of
endurance, be he "elite" athlete or "miserable" specimen.

The heart rate should return to 110-120 beats per minute or below
during the rest interval and should not exceed 144 (24 x 6) beats
per minute during early training (see Chapter 6—The Exercise
Program, on 70% levels).

Specific warm-up

Continuous, specific warm-up is needed particularly for running or
cardiovascular work in order to aid in the demand for oxygen by
the heart, lungs, and active muscles. It is through this interval
training, time-conscious warm-up that the small blood vessels and
capillaries of the heart's coronary circulation open and meet the
oxygen demand. The same dilation or opening of vessels occurs in
the lungs and contracting muscles.

The early flexibility or Phase I, Preparatory Period, readies the
joints and musculo-skeletal tissue for the Phase II, Cardiovascular
Period. However, it only partially prepares the cardio-respiratory
system and active muscles for this second phase. Again we see the
specificity of exercise in performing its function. Additional warm-
up time of approximately 5-10 minutes is needed to ready the body
functions for the circulatory demands of Phase II.

Concentrate on cardiovascular

Don't neglect the musculo-skeletal systems, but remember the first
aim is cardiovascular. See Chapter 5 for the purposes of the
"Exercise Program." It is coronary heart disease which is killing

45

us at the rate of over one-half million annually in the United States. If given an opportunity, the cardiovascular system will adjust, but you must perform specific cardiovascular work to make changes. Weight training and musculo-endurance work will *not* do it. Continuous, rhythmic cardiovascular exercise include running, cycling, rowing, swimming, skipping, and hiking. Increase the Heart Rate to 60% of working capacity from 0-3 months and 70% from 4-6 months, and thereafter.

Individualize programs and gradually increase dosage.

Each adult is an entity and must be scheduled with a specific program, particularly in the Phase II, Cardiovascular period. It is impossible to place men into large running groups after the early months of training. They need to be individualized by designing a special program and dosage for each man. At the most, perhaps two or three men can be given similar workout routines, but *no more*. Many gradations occur in a large mass of men. Thus, some may overdo and others underdo. Each must perform at about 70 percent of his maximum capacity, depending upon his exercise tolerance or related medical-physical factors. Others may be maintained at a lower or higher level of energy output. *Don't leave it to chance*. Exercise is "specific" and not a "cure-all" or general therapeutic agent. It must be individually specified for each person.

Monthly exercise schedules are successfully used in the San Diego State Adult Fitness Program. These schedules are designed by the leaders.

Gradually increasing the exercise "dosage," thereby causing the body to adapt or meet the new demand, is a very old method of improving various body functions. This includes endurance, strength, agility, and flexibility. This method or law is known as the "overload" principle (69).

Phase I, Preparatory—should start with low intensity and gradually increase, but the repetitions remain relatively small, i.e., 10-15 per exercise.

Phase II, Cardiovascular—starts with a low intensity, but a high number of repetitions. Intensity increases with time and exercise tolerance, and repetitions remain high. Intensity seldom is great in cardiovascular endurance training.

46

Do Not Sprint during cardiovascular work. **Keep intensity relatively low and duration long (a minmum of 15 minutes).**

Follow trunk hyperextension with trunk flexion

Trunk hypextension exercises may be contra-indicated in middle-aged men and women. This is particularly true of persons suffering from "low back syndrome." When trunk hyperextension exercises are used, they should be done cautiously and judiciously. In addition, to relieve any possible low back strain or muscle spasm, they should always be followed by a trunk flexion or a combination exercise of trunk flexion with rotation, and preferably of a "non-weight bearing" variety. A good example of this is exercise No. 13, a back hyper-extensor, followed by No. 14, a low back flexor.

Good leadership

Although self-motivated fitness programs are to be commended and are the eventual goal, men are best trained under *competent leaders*. One must first learn to exercise, know his capabilities, and develop a real understanding of exercise principles before embarking on his or her own program. Exercise for adults is a new branch of learning or discipline which must be respected as such. Most physical educators need additional, extra training in learning how to exercise adults.

Competent leaders are of inestimable value

Group exercises directed by a well-trained leader-instructor are (1) easier to follow, (2) become more enjoyable, (3) eliminate overdoing, (4) create fewer mistakes and are more pedagogically correct, (5) demand less mental effort and self-motivation, and (6) are usually more valuable to the participants.

Avoid Isometrics

Isometric exercising is a method of contracting the muscles against a fixed load such as an immovable bar. It is usually performed for six seconds. It has become a fad for developing strength as originally claimed by Hettinger and Mueller of Germany (41). Recently (2, 84) it has been found only slightly if at all effective in increasing strength.

Isometrics are contra-indicated with Middle-Aged Adults

Increase in movement for the development of cardiovascular function is the main purpose of fitness programs for middle-aged adults.

47

Isometric contraction prevents circulation and blood flow through the muscles by compressing the arteries (14) (36) (83) (96). The flow of blood through a muscle is enhanced by alternate rhythmic contraction (83).

> **BODY MOVEMENT IS FUN—move for fun and *greater blood flow* and cardiovascular improvement.**

Regularity

Regular exercise is a *must. Spasmodic exercise may be dangerous.* Possible increase in the clotting mechanism appears to occur with sporadic physical activity (22). *Most exercise benefits cannot be stored.* The daily-regular renewal of the stimuli causing adaptation is essential to the continual effects of physical activity. Just as food intake is used up almost daily so are the benefits of exercise unless they are replenished with *more* exercise.

In twelve months of regular training, nine middle-aged males in the San Diego State Adult Fitness Program made a 20 percent improvement in their circulatory function as determined by Oxygen Uptake Studies. No change was seen in the six non-exercising control subjects. The exercising subjects were on a three-day per week regimen. Those making the greatest gain were the most regular in attendance and spent the greatest amount of time exercising (about 12 miles per week).

Taper-off and relax

"Taper-off" is obligatory after cardiovascular work in particular, but also after any type of vigorous exercise. This permits the body systems and metabolic processes to return to near normal. It should include walking, jogging, and flexibility movement. Continuous running causes some tightness in the joints, particularly of the lumbar spine. Release of tension in the muscles is accomplished by range of motion and flexibility exercises for several minutes after running has ceased. If possible, an additional ten-minute swim is helpful and relaxing.

The physiological value of the return of the metabolic processes is readily seen; the psychological values are very helpful to the continued enthusiasm of the regularly exercising adult.

NEVER END WITH A SPRINT

The demand for increase stroke volume caused by sprinting is probably too great for most middle-aged persons and should *always be avoided*. Sprints are anaerobic and therefore build up too great an oxygen debt for most adults to tolerate. This sudden great demand for blood and oxygen is likely to be beyond the cardiac reserve of many hearts of the middle-aged with possible catastrophic results.

Avoid over-fatigue

Some fatigue is essential to the improvement of the body's physiological function through exercise. It creates an adaptation so that more improvement can occur. When the body is exercised over a period of time, a greater demand for oxygen develops, which in turn creates an O_2 debt. It is this debt at an optimal level which helps improve cardiovascular function.

The great running coach Lydiard says, *"Train, don't strain."* After the taper-off from exercise, one should be able to exercise again immediately. If not, he is *"straining."*

Again, remember that *time is in your favor*, permit it to work to your favor.

Chapter 6

THE EXERCISE PROGRAM
(HOW TO EXERCISE)
(STAGES I, II AND III)

Preparatory to vigorous exercising is a preliminary period called "warm-up" or "readiness" (69). The body tissue of middle-aged persons (males in particular) is usually less elastic than in former years and needs careful stretching and adapting. Heating up the body and increasing the metabolism, stretching tight ligamentous and connective (collagen) tissue, getting the joints ready for movement, relaxing, increasing heart and lung action, and improving the body coordination and motor patterns, all play an important role in this preliminary-preparation period. This is best accomplished during the first three months of training (Stage I) by alternating the prepartory exercises with the cardio-vascular exercises (Phases I and II). During the fourth and fifth months (Stage II—intermediate) the training is divided into two 30-minute phases (30-30 Program). Stage III, Advanced Fitness, is likewise divided into two 30-minute phases, but greater latitude is permitted the trainee.

Often people ask, "Should I run?" *Yes,* but remember that you run with your musclo-skeletal system; your joints and muscles. Therefore, prepare them for the running. *DON'T NEGLECT THE VERY TISSUE* which carries you about as you run to develop your cardiovascular-respiratory system. Remember your feet, too, (53).

The key to success in exercising adults is the use of "interval training." Work-rest. The body can adapt to work if the rest period is long enough to permit the performer to accommodate to the exercise before starting again. The Heart Rate should be below 110-120 during the rest interval before resuming work. In addition, trunk hyperextension should be used cautiously and always followed by trunk flexion or lateral movements.

THIS CHAPTER IS DIVIDED AS FOLLOWS:

Stage I —**Beginning Fitness (5-10 Program)**—**First three months**
Stage II —**Intermediate Fitness (30-30) Program**—**4th and 5th months**

Stage III—Advanced Fitness (30-30 Program)—6 months and thereafter
Supplemental Programs—Phase I and II

EXERCISE PROGRAMS

Program for First Three Months

STAGE I: BEGINNING FITNESS (the 5-10 program)
Do Exercises 1 through 10 in the first 10 minute period
Run for five minutes
Do exercises 11 through 20 in next ten minute period
Run for five minutes
Do exercises 21 through 30 in next ten minutes period
Run for 5 minutes

Program for Months Four and Five

STAGE II: INTERMEDIATE FITNESS (the 30-30 program)
PHASE I: PREPARATORY EXERCISES FOR 30 MINUTES
(do exercises 31 through 60)
PHASE II: CARDIOVASCULAR FITNESS
(by running and walking; or by swimming, cycling, rowing, rope skipping, cross country running, cross country skiing, skating, vigorous hiking)

For Next Six Months of Training and Thereafter

PHASE I: PREPARATORY EXERCISES FOR 30 MINUTES
(do exercises 61 through 90)
PHASE II: CARDIOVASCULAR FITNESS
(by running and walking; or by swimming, cycling, rowing rope skipping, cross country running, cross country skiing, skating, vigorous hiking)

Supplemental Programs for Next Six Months and Thereafter

SUPPLEMENTAL EXERCISE PROGRAM A; OR SUPPLE-MENTAL EXERCISE PROGRAM B; OR SUPPLEMENTAL EXERCISE PROGRAM C
CARDIOVASCULAR FITNESS
(by running and walking, or by swimming, cycling, rowing, rope skipping, cross country running, cross country skiing, skating, vigorous hiking)

OTHER SUPPLEMENTAL PROGRAMS: RUNNING PRO-GRAM; RUN FOR FUN PROGRAM; 1, 2, 3, PROGRAM; 10, 10, 10, PROGRAM; 15 MINUTE PROGRAM; DISTANCE PROGRAM; 440 PROGRAM; 880 PROGRAM; DESIGN YOUR OWN PROGRAM

These programs are devised for most middle-aged Americans. However, it must be remembered that great individual differences exist. Start at Stage I and progress at your own rate. Use the suggested guidelines for graduation to the next stage. Don't hurry. *TIME IS IN YOUR FAVOR.*

STAGE I
BEGINNING FITNESS (The 5-10 Program)
THE FIRST THREE MONTHS

Follow the order or sequence of exercises explicitly. *Do Not Vary Them* and *Don't Omit Any.* There are a total of thirty exercises with periods of running every 10 minutes. Perform the exercise rhythmically and with ease of movement. Breathing Pattern— Exhale on effort or during contraction. Note instructions. Background music adds to the enjoyment and rhythm of exercising. The instructor must show enthusiasm.

#1—*ARM CIRCLING*

Move the arms so that the shoulder joint is moved through a 360° rotation in both planes. *Breath freely* and accentuate exhalation as each arm gets to the bottom of the rotation.

REPETITIONS,   1-6 WEEKS = 20 IN EACH PLANE
                          7-12 WEEKS = 30 IN EACH PLANE

1a   1b

#2—TRUNK LATERAL BENDING

(a) Starting position: stand with arms sideward at shoulder level
(b) Flex trunk directly sideward to right, dropping right arm to side, *exhale*
(c) Return to starting position
(d) Repeat to right
There are a total of 4 counts per cycle

REPETITIONS,   1-6 WEEKS = 5 L and 5 R (20 COUNTS)
                    7-12 WEEKS = 10 L and 10 R (40 counts)

2

#3—*LEG RAISING* (forward, sideward, rearward)

(a) Standing position, raise left leg forward, *exhale*, and lower
(b) Repeat with right leg
(c) Raise right leg sideward, *exhale*, and lower
(d) Repeat with left leg
(e) Raise right leg rearward, lower trunk forward and touching hands to floor, *exhale* and return to standing
(f) Repeat with left leg

REPETITIONS,   1-6 WEEKS = 30 (10 EACH POSITION)
                      7-12 WEEKS = 45 (15 EACH POSITION)

3a   3b

3c

#4—KNEE PRESSER

Lie supine, lift left knee to chest, press close to chest with hands and *exhale*. Repeat with right knee. Keep all posterior surface as close to floor as possible.

REPETITIONS, 1-6 WEEKS = 10
7-12 WEEKS = 16

4

#5—NECK ROTATION

Rotate head to the right around vertical axis 360°. Reverse direction to the left every two repetitions. *Exhale* in forward position.

REPETITIONS, 1-6 WEEKS = 10
7-12 WEEKS = 16

5

#6—*BACK ROCKER* (ON MAT)

Assume a sitting position on floor, tuck lower extremities close to chest and clasp knees with both hands. Rock backward and *exhale*, then forward and inhale. Continue as a rocking chair.

REPETITIONS, 1-6 WEEKS = 5
7-12 WEEKS = 10

6a

6b

#7—*THE WRINGER*

Lie on back with arms outstretched to side at shoulder level. Carefully kick the right foot to left hand, *exhale*. Kick the left foot to right hand, *exhale*. Turn the head opposite to the kick.

REPETITIONS, 1-6 WEEKS = 5L, 5R
7-12 WEEKS = 10L, 10R

7a

7b

#8—KNEEL AND STRETCH

Start on all fours in kneeling position. Lift right leg rearward to horizontal position with knee straight, inhale. Bring knee forward and force fully to chest, *exhale*, and lower knee to floor. Repeat with left limb.

REPETITIONS, 1-6 WEEKS = 5L, 5R
7-12 WEEKS = 10L, 10R

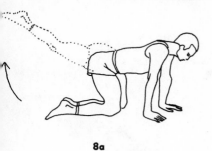

8a

8b

#9—SLEEPING BEAUTY

Lie on right side with head resting on right forearm and neck in line with the spine. Kick left leg forward and swing left arm rearward parallel with the floor, *exhale*. Swing left leg rearward and left arm forward overhead and inhale. Repeat on left side.

REPETITIONS, 1-6 WEEKS = 5L, 5R
7-12 WEEKS = 10L, 10R

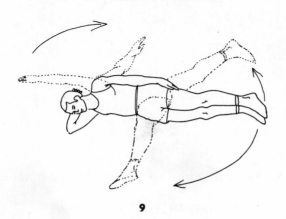

9

#10—*FOOT CIRCLES*

Stand with hands on wall and feet 12-14 inches apart. Rotate on periphery of the feet in a circular motion to the left (counter-clockwise). Repeat each two circles to right. *Exhale freely.*

REPETITIONS,   1-6 WEEKS = 4R, 4L
                7-12 WEEKS = 10R, 10L

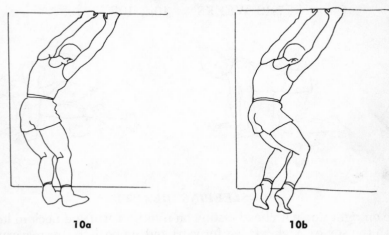

10a   10b

FIRST FIVE MINUTE RUNNING PERIOD

The Running phase consists of alternately running and walking with *exhalation accentuated* through-out. Running is performed on the whole foot with a forward rolling motion and push off.

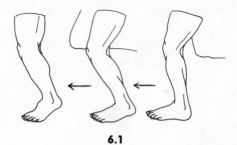

6.1

FIG. 6.1, MECHANICS OF RUNNING FOR ADULTS

DO NOT RUN ON THE TOES
(leg soreness and foot problems result)

FIRST FIVE MINUTE RUNNING PERIOD

Running should be done in a small circle or oval with an approximate radius of 20-50 feet so that the instructor-leader can watch all of the participants for running skill, pallor, excessive dyspnea, or undue fatigue. Obese persons usually have more difficulty than those of normal weight (make allowances).

Run 15 seconds, walk 45 seconds—1 minute

" 15 " " 45 " —1 minute

" 20 " " 40 " —1 minute

" 20 " " 40 " —1 minute

" 20 " " 40 " —1 minute

Total=5 minutes

CAUTION—A word about breathing = *Exhale* on effort. *AVOID BREATH HOLDING.* Follow the directions of exhaltion found under each exercise description. Heart rates should be checked for 10 seconds and remain below 144/min. Teach the subjects to count their own pulses.

RESUME EXERCISING

#11—CALF STRETCHER

Place one foot ahead of the other about two feet in a stride position with the forward knee flexed and the rear one extended. Lean trunk forward until a continuous stretch occurs to the rear calf, hold for 15 seconds. Change leg positions. Breathe freely.

REPETITIONS, 1-6 WEEKS = 4

7-12 WEEKS = 6

11a

11b

#12—HIP MASSAGER

Lie on right side with arms outstretched overhead. Pull both knees to chest, *exhale*. Return to outstretched position. Turn over to left side and repeat exercise.

REPETITIONS, 1-6 WEEKS = 5L, 5R
        7-12 WEEKS = 7L, 7R

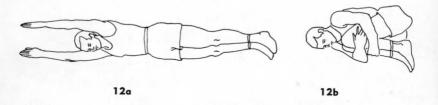

12a   12b

#13—CHEST RAISER

Lie prone (face down) arms at shoulder level. Raise the trunk and arms at shoulder level. Raise the trunk and arms from the floor keeping chin down and neck flat, inhale. Return to floor and *exhale*. *DO NOT PERMIT FEET TO LIFT FROM FLOOR.*

REPETITIONS, 1-6 WEEKS = 5
        7-12 WEEKS = 8

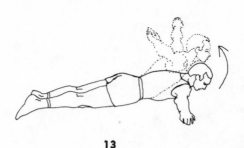

13

#14—*LOW BACK STRETCHER*

Lie prone with hands palms down at shoulder level in push-up position. Push arms and straighten keeping weight on knees and bending hips until buttocks nearly touch heels, *exhale*. Return to prone position and inhale.

REPETITIONS, 1-6 WEEKS = 5
7-12 WEEKS = 10

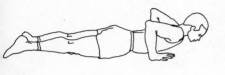

14a

14b

#15—*ARM STRETCHER*

Rotate arm from shoulder joint keeping elbow straight. *Exhale* on downward motion. Move through two planes.

REPETITIONS, 1-6 WEEKS = 10
7-12 WEEKS = 16

15

#16—MAD CAT

Start on all fours, lift back upward in a stretched, arched position *exhale*. Return to original position, inhale.

REPETITIONS, 1-6 WEEKS = 5
7-12 WEEKS = 8

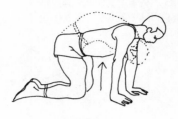

16

#17—LYING SIDE LEG RAISER

Lie on left side with head resting comfortably on forearm and in line with spine. Raise right leg laterally, Inhale. Lower and *exhale*. Repeat on right side.

REPETITIONS, 1-6 WEEKS = 5L, 5R
7-12 WEEKS = 10L, 10R

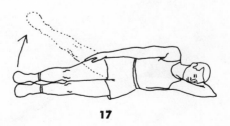

17

#18—SPLIT STRETCHER

Standing feet spread 3'-4', bend left knee keeping weight over left foot and hands on left knee. Stretch right thigh. Keep right foot flat on deck (to avoid knee stretch), *exhale*. Repeat to right side.

REPETITIONS,   1-6   WEEKS = 4L, 4R
                 7-12 WEEKS = 8L, 8R

18

#19—ONE-HALF KNEE BENDS

Stand with feet parallel, lower body by bending knees in a *half squat* keeping *heels on floor*. *Exhale* and return to original standing position. Avoid full knee bends.

REPETITIONS,   1-6   WEEKS = 5
                 7-12 WEEKS = 10

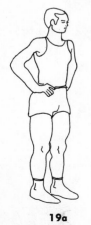

19a

19b

#20—EASY BRIDGE

Lie on back with feet near buttocks. Lift the hips off floor using feet and shoulders for support, inhaling until reaching the top. *Exhale* throughout the lowering movement.

REPETITIONS, 1-6 WEEKS = 4
7-12 WEEKS = 8

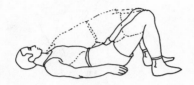

20

SECOND FIVE MINUTE RUNNING PERIOD

Concentrate on running form and ease of running along with rhythmic breathing. Again alternately run and walk.

Run	15	seconds,	walk	45	seconds—1	minute
"	20	"	"	40	"	1 "
"	20	"	"	40	"	1 "
"	20	"	"	40	"	1 "
"	25	"	"	35	"	1 "

TOTAL: 5 minutes

Again count heart rates for 10 seconds and maintain them below 144/min. *RESUME EXERCISING*

#21—ABDOMINAL CHURN

Stand with feet 15" apart, hands on hips. Lower trunk sideward to left and continue to forward postion, *exhale*. Continue rotation to right and return to upright position, inhale. Repeat and reverse direction each two revolutions or rotations.

REPETITIONS,   1-6 WEEKS = 10
                    7-12 WEEKS = 16

21

#22—ELBOW SUPPORT, KNEE PRESSER

Rest supinely on elbows. Flex left knee to chest, *exhale*. Repeat to right alternately.

REPETITIONS,   1-6 WEEKS = 5L, 5R
                    7-12 WEEKS = 10L, 10R

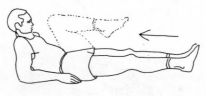

22

#23—*ARM CIRCLING ON KNEES WITH TRUNK LOWERING*

Start on knees. Simultaneously rotate left arm counterclockwise and right arm clockwise each in a 360° motion. Bend body forward as arms are lowered, *exhale,* and straighten body as arms are overhead. Reverse rotation.

REPETITIONS, 1-6 WEEKS = 10
7-12 WEEKS = 20

 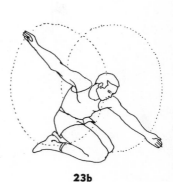

23a   23b

#24—*HALF-SIT UPS*

Lie on back (supine) arms at sides. Move to half sitting position, sliding hands to knees and twist to left, exhale. Return to lying position. Repeat with twist to right.

REPETITIONS, 1-6 WEEKS = 6
7-12 WEEKS = 10

24

#25—FLOOR ROLLING

Lie on back, arms outstretched on floor overhead. Roll to right
onto chest and abdomen and *exhale;* reverse roll to left onto back,
inhale; continue to left and *exhale;* reverse to back and inhale.

REPETITIONS, 1-6 WEEKS = 6
　　　　　　　 7-12 WEEKS = 10

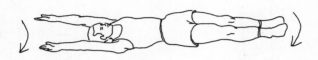

25a

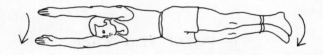

25b

25c

#26—TOE RAISING AND RUN IN PLACE

Rise up on toes, inhale; lower to heels, *exhale*. Run in place ten repetitions. Again rise on toes and run in place.

REPETITIONS, 1-6 WEEKS = 5
                 7-12 WEEKS = 10

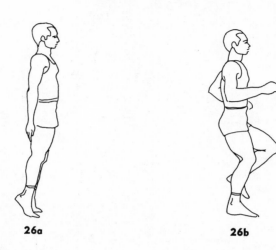

26a   **26b**

#27—INSTEP STRETCHER

Start in standing position with legs spread three feet. Twist body to left and roll over right toe and instep (dorsum), *exhale*. Repeat to right side.

REPETITIONS, 1-6 WEEKS = 4L, 4R
                 7-12 WEEKS = 8L, 8R

27

#28—*ANKLE STRETCHER*

Stand with hands on wall at chest height with feet together and four feet distance from the wall. Alternately flex one knee and *exhale*. The opposite calf and hamstring group are in stretch.

REPETITIONS,   1-6 WEEKS = 5L, 5R
                     7-12 WEEKS = 8L, 8R

This exercise can be accomplished without a wall by standing in a stride position.

28

#29—*TOE TOUCHER WITH LEG SHAKING*

Stand with arms outstretched overhead. Lower trunk forward and touch toes, *exhale*. Return to standing position, inhale and shake legs.

REPETITIONS,   1-6 WEEKS = 4
                     7-12 WEEKS = 8

29a

29b

#30—SUPINE REST

Lie on back with knees flexed and together, feet apart and toe adducted or turned in. Arms at side or hands on chest. *Exhale* forcefully and ventilate. This may be modified by head rotation clockwise and counter clockwise, 360°, followed by lowering head to floor and *exhaling*. 1-3 minute duration.

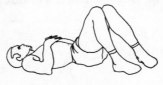

30

THIRD FIVE MINUTE RUNNING PERIOD

Remember—Run on whole foot and *Exhale, Exhale!*

Run	15	seconds, walk	45	seconds—	1	minute
”	20	”	”	40	”	1	”
”	20	”	”	40	”	1	”
”	25	”	”	35	”	1	”
”	30	”	”	30	”	1	”

TOTAL: 5 minutes

Count heart rates and keep them below 144/min. If rates are too low, increase the running time.

Taper Off with 3 minutes walking and stretching, followed by 3-5 repetitions of the foregoing exercise numbers 1, 2, 5, 10, 11, 21, 27, 28, and 29. Always "Taper Off". Bring the body functions back to near resting conditions. Heart rate below 110-120.

Running tends to stiffen the muscles and ligaments of the spine and legs. Therefore, it is imperative that it be followed by flexibility and stretching exercise. *Release Tension, Relax!*

GRADUATION REQUIREMENTS

to move to Stage II include:

1. **Kasch Pulse Recovery Test, Heart Rate below 130, First Recovery Minute**
2. **Run continuously two minutes**
3. **Heart Rate 2 minutes after the 2-minute run is 120 or below (20 x 6)**

STAGE II
INTERMEDIATE FITNESS (30-30 PROGRAM)
THE 4TH AND 5TH MONTHS

By the fourth month, the trainee generally is ready for an increase in exercise intensity of both a preparatory and cardiovascular nature. This is accomplished by dividing the exercise into two distinct phases: I, Preparatory and II, Cardiovascular. Each phase is 30 minutes in duration and thus is named the 30-30 Program.

Careful allowance should be made for individual differences, particularly in Phase II, Cardiovascular. After three months' training, all persons should have a one-minute recovery heart rate below 130 on the Kasch Pulse Recovery Test prior to starting Stage II. See chapter on "Testing and Evaluation."

Remember, follow the exercise sequence.
DO NOT SHORTCUT ANY PORTION
(Get your joints, ligaments, and muscles ready for the running)

STAGE II—PHASE (I)—PREPARATORY EXERCISES, 30 MINUTES

#31—ARM ROTATION

Rotate the arms alternately and raise the feet reciprocally in a slight kicking action, breath freely, accentuating the *exhale*.
REPETITIONS = 20

31

#32—*TRUNK TWISTING*

With hands in neck firm position, fingers interlocked, twist trunk to right, *exhale*. Repeat alternately to left.

REPETITIONS = 5-10L, 5-10R

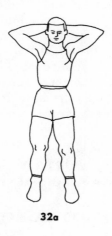

32a

32b

#33—*EAR PRESSER*

Lie on back, press right hand against right ear and resist. Left arm at side position on floor. Repeat with left hand.

REPETITIONS = 4L, 4R

33

#34—DOUBLE KNEE PRESSER

Lie on back arms to side pull both knees to chest and clamp with forearms and hands, *exhale* and continue to *exhale* slowly as feet are replaced on floor and arms return overhead, inhale.

REPETITIONS = 10

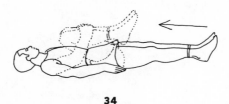

34

#35—NECK ROTATION, SITTING

Rotate head clockwise 360°, *exhale* in forward position and inhale in rear position. Reverse direction alternately.

REPETITIONS = 4L, 4R

35

#36—DOUBLE WRINGER

Lie on back with arms outstretched sideward at shoulder level. Kick right foot to left hand, *exhale*. Release kick slightly and kick again, *exhale*. Turn head to opposite side of kick. Repeat alternately to right.

REPETITIONS =5-10L, 5-10R

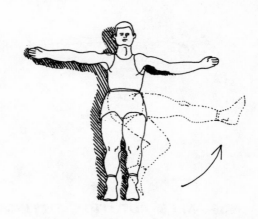

36a

36b

#37—CHIN STRETCHER

Start in "all fours" position on hands and knees. (1) Lift right knee forward to chest, *exhale;* (2) Lift right leg rearward horizontal, inhale; (3) Swing right leg forward and laterally keeping knee straight and touching floor with foot, *exhale;* (4) Return right leg to rear horizontal position, inhale; (5) forcefully bring right knee to chest, *exhale;* (6) Return knee to floor, inhale. Repeat the 6 counts using left leg.

REPETITIONS = 5R, 5L

37a

37b

37c

37d

#38—ANKLE ROLLS, SITTING

Sitting position, rotate ankles in 360° circle clockwise, using full range of motion.

REPETITIONS = 10

38

#39—RUN IN PLACE

Run in place, raising knees until they are horizontal. Continue one minute.

39

#40—CALF AND FOOT STRETCHER

Stand in stride position with forward knee partially flexed and
rear one full extended. Lean trunk forward until a continuous
stretch occurs to the rear calf, *exhale*. Then dip front knee and
roll rear foot over instep (dorsum), *exhale*. Next, turn body 180
degrees and repeat the exercise.

REPETITIONS = 5L, 5R

40a

40b

#41—FLUTTER KICK

Lie prone with chin resting on hands palms down. With knees
extended alternately kick legs with feet moving about 6 inches.
Breathe freely throughout.

REPETITIONS = 10-15

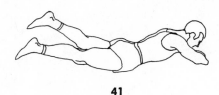

41

#42—KNEE PUSH UP

Lie prone on floor with palms down under shoulders. Push up with arms bending left hip and knee, but extending right leg rearward until buttocks touches left heel, *exhale*. Return to prone position and repeat with left leg extended.

REPETITIONS = 5-10

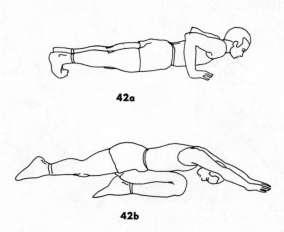

42a

42b

#43—HIP TWISTER

Lie on back, hands in neck firm position, knees drawn to chest. Roll legs and thighs to left side, keeping knees together, and touching floor, *exhale*. Return to starting position, inhale and repeat to right.

REPETITIONS = 5L, 5R

43a   43b

#44—BENT KNEE, SIT UP

Lie supine with knees flexed and feet flat on floor about one foot from buttocks, arms extended overhead. Come to a sitting position throwing the arms forward and twisting to the left, *exhale*. Return to supine position and repeat to right.

REPETITIONS = 5-10

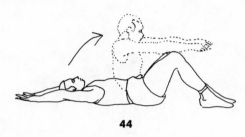

44

#45—SINGLE KNEE BEND

Standing position. Bend left knee one-half keeping heel down and slightly raise right foot from floor. Repeat twice. *Exhale* at bottom. Repeat twice with right knee.

REPETITIONS = 6-8L, 6-8R

45

#46—SIDE DANCER

Start in standing position. Kick left leg to left side and simultaneously double hop on right foot, *exhale*. Continue to right side in a rhythmical manner.

REPETITIONS = 10L, 10R

46

#47—SCALE

Start standing with arms extended overhead. Lower trunk forward and touch hands to floor, simultaneously raising right leg to rear horizontal position, *exhale*. Return to standing, inhale, and repeat to opposite side.

REPETITIONS = 5L, 5R

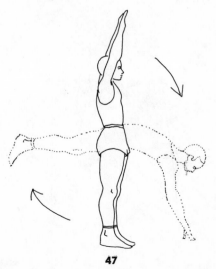

47

#48—PRONE ROCK

Lie prone with arms outstreched sideward. Rock to right side raising left arm, inhale. Rock to left side, *exhale*, at mid point on belly
and inhale as left arm is raised.

REPETITIONS = 5L, 5R

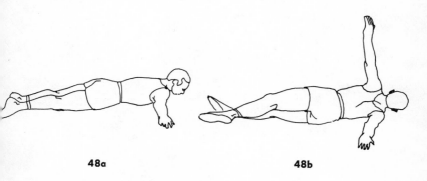

48a   48b

#49—BACK BENDER

Sitting on floor in tuck position roll back with legs tucked and
straighten knees, touching floor with left foot, *exhale*. Roll forward
and inhale, then back again and touch right foot to floor, *exhale*.

REPETITIONS = 8

49a   49b

#50—*ABDOMINAL PRESSER*

Lie on back, lift both legs to vertical, *exhale*. Flex knees to chest and return feet to floor, inhale.

REPETITIONS = 10

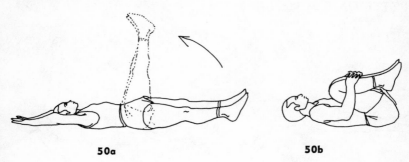

50a   50b

#51—*PLUNGER*

From standing position, lunge forward with left foot and thrust arms to sideward shoulder level position, *exhale*. Return to standing and repeat with right foot.

REPETITIONS = 5L, 5R

51

tanding, hands at sides. Lower trunk half forward and simul-
aneously swing arms forward in front of body, *exhale*. Continue
he motion bringing arms rearward and upward, to a position level
vith shoulders, raise trunk to upright position and return hands to
ides, inhale.

REPETITIONS = 10

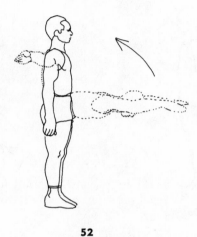

52

#53—SIX COUNT BURPEE

Standing position. (1) Come to full squat hands on floor outside of knees, *exhale*. (2) Jump and extend to front support, inhale (3) Dip down, *exhale*. (4) Push up, inhale. (5) Jump to squat *exhale*. (6) Stand, inhale.

REPETITIONS = 5-8

53a 53b

53c

53d

#54—*WINDMILL*

Standing position hands clasped overhead. Turn trunk left and flex touching floor outside of left foot, *exhale*. Return to standing and repeat to right side.

REPETITIONS = 5L, 5R

54

#55—*ELBOW LEG RAISER*

Lying half supine with part of weight resting on the elbows, raise the left leg with knee straight, *exhale*. Repeat consecutively 10-20 times with each leg.

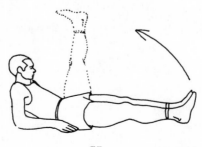

55

#56—ENDURANCE HOPS

Continuous hopping starting with left foot (5 repetitions), right foot (5), both feet (10), straddle hop (15), stride hop (15) for a total of 50 hops. Repeat for 100 repetitions when the legs and feet develop more tolerance. *Exhale* on each hop.

56a

56b

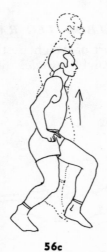

56c

#57—STRADDLE TOE TOUCH

Stand with feet spread 36 inches and hands clasped overhead. Bend forward and touch hands to left foot, *exhale*. Repeat to right side.

REPETITIONS = 5L, 5R

57

#58—THIGH AND HAMSTRING STRETCHER

Standing position. Bend right knee, grasp right foot, and pull to rear with resulting stretch on front of right thigh, inhale. Lower right foot to floor and flex trunk, touch toes and *exhale*. Repeat exercise with left foot and leg.

REPETITIONS = 5L, 5R

58a

58b

#59—BRIDGE

Lie supine with feet close to buttocks and hands in inverted push up position. Arch back and place weight on back of head and hands, *exhale* slowly and lower back to floor. Variation = rolling slightly left and right.
REPETITIONS = 5

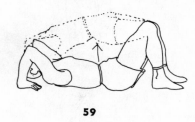

59

#60—SUPINE REST WITH NECK ROTATION

Lie supine in physiological rest position. Knees are bent, feet apart with heels out and toes turned in. Back flat on deck, hands clasped across lower chest. Flex head forward, rotate head clockwise, then counterclockwise, and lower to floor, *exhale* freely. Roll head from side to side. Repeat two or three times until muscle tension eases.

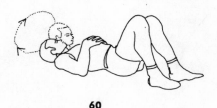

60

STAGE II—PHASE (II)—CARDIOVASCULAR FITNESS
30 MINUTES

4TH AND 5TH MONTHS OF TRAINING

The "30-30 Program" calls for 30 minutes of cardiovascular exercise following Phase I, the Preparatory Period. This is usually accomplished by running and walking, but may be substituted by swimming, cycling, rowing, rope skipping, cross-country skiing, orienteering, hiking, and skating. Running is first choice for the following reasons: (1) It can be done alone or with others, (2) No equipment is needed, (3) It can be done at one's own rate of speed, (4) It can be done throughout a lifetime, (5) Either sex can do it, (6) Little danger is involved, and (7) It can be carefully graded in intensity and duration.

How Much Running?

It is imperative that the cardiovascular system be called upon for greater output in a very careful and gradual manner. One must control this by his heart rate and not by competing with his neighbor or friends. Each person's running program should be graded. Karvonen (46) has given us a very excellent and safe method of determining the heart rate for running. Suppose a man is 45 years of age with a resting heart rate of 70 beats per minute. His maximum heart rate is approximately 175 beats per minute. The following formula is used:

Max. HR − Resting HR × 70% + Resting HR = Exercise Level
Example:

$$\begin{array}{ll} \text{Maximum HR} = 175 & 105 \\ & 70\% \\ \text{Resting HR} = 70 & \overline{73.50} \\ & +70 \\ \text{Difference} = 105 & \overline{143.5} \end{array}$$

The working heart rate is 144 and the 10 second count would be 24 ($24 \times 6 = 144$). This is the maximum rate or exercise level that each man should attempt to reach. Below is a table of average heart rates from several sources. Howevers, it must be noted that there is considerable individual variation. Resting heart rates normally range from 50-100 with the average about 70 per minute according to Best and Taylor (18). Maximum heart rates usually are lower than those shown in Table 6.1 and resting rates higher.

TABLE 6.1

MAXIMUM HEART RATES AND BASAL RESTING HEART RATES OF MALE SUBJECTS BY AGE*

SOURCE	Age 20-30	Age 31-40	Age 41-50	Age 51-60	Age 61+
Maximal Heart Rates					
Astrand, I. *Acta. Phys. Sc.*, 1960	186	181	173	161	159
Robinson, S., *Arbeitsphys.*, 1938	197	206	184	185	176
Kasch, F., et al.	190	187	185	178	
Basal Heart Rates					
Robinson, S., *Arbeitsphys.*, 1938	62	57	61	62	58

*Great individual variations occur in Heart Rates

Care must be used in outlining the running programs for each man. Men between 30-60 years with heart rates after three months' training over 130 on the Kasch Pulse Recovery Test (see Chapter 4) should be kept at a slow pace. This advice holds for those with hypertension, obesity, excessively high heart rates (tachycardia), and various pathologies.

Generally the heart rate for most middle-aged men (30-60) should remain below 150 (25 x 6) during the 4th and 5th months of training.

Mechanics of Running

Remember—*WHEN YOU RUN*, the entire foot should make contact with the surface with a rolling motion and continue with a push off.

Run in Groups

As running is usually best performed in groups, it is an excellent procedure to divide your group into three subdivisions. Each division should have a leader. The running phase should be started with 50 running and 50 walking steps and continue for 20 to 30 minutes. Rest periods may be needed. The three divisions will be separated with the better trained runners in the lead, next in second place, and those in poor condition third. As fitness improves, 30 minutes is necessary.

Heart Rate

Heart Rates should be counted every two minutes using the 10 second counting procedure. The rates should remain below 144-150 per minute (24 or 25/10 sec.). The leaders of the three divisions should record the heart rates. Adjustments should be made within the sub-divisions in accordance with the heart rate findings. If heart rates elevate beyond 150 per minute, the man should be slowed down by placing him in a slower division. If it is at 132 or 138 per minute, he should be increased in pace and sent up to a slightly faster group. As the divisions progress, the running duration increases and the rest decreases, so long as the Heart Rate remains below 150 and returns to below 120 before resuming running.

Caution:

Men with excessive fatigue, weakness, pallor, dyspnea, fainting tendency, low pulse pressure or high diastolic blood pressure during the running or immediately thereafter, should be referred to their own physician for reevaluation. If they are again cleared by their physicians, they should be placed on individualized running regimens and carefully monitored.

The Heart Rate should return to below 110-120 per minute during the rest interval before resuming running. Usually this occurs within two minutes. This should not be assumed, but actually checked by the leader. Remember, it only takes 10 seconds for a HR check. *DO NOT* start the work interval until the rate is below 120 per minute.

The heart rate is a practical means of controlling work output (8,46), but it does *not* always reflect the work of the heart. It is only a good estimate. When coupled with other findings, such as ECG, O_2 uptake, O_2 pulse, cardiac output, and blood pressure, it is more valuable.

GRADUATION REQUIREMENTS

to move to Stage III include:

1. Kasch Pulse Recovery Test, Heart Rate below 120, First Recovery Minute
2. Run 5 minutes continuously
3. Heart Rate 2 minutes after the 5-minute run, 120 or below (20 x 6)

STAGE III

ADVANCED FITNESS (30-30 PROGRAM)
SIX MONTHS OF TRAINING AND THEREAFTER

The program at the sixth month of training continues to be divided into two 30 minute periods, Phase I and Phase II. A complete program is given and several others suggested. It is recommended that most participants follow the three stages as outlined and *not* to vary Stage III until after one year. If this should occur after a year one should again review the principles and sequence of exercises prior to proceeding. Or better yet, get the advice of an expert.

Caution:

It is easy to be lulled into thinking that running is the best single kind of exercise. *No one exercise type is best.* Some types are preferred over others. Running generally is the best kind of exercise for cardiovascular fitness. Although swimming or cycling may be best for some adults. Whether you run, swim, or cycle for cardiovascular fitness you must use muscles, bones, and joints to propel yourself. *The greatest single problem* occurring in adults who exercise *is musculoskeletal problems* causing joint, muscle, and bone aches and pains. Sometimes they persist for a few weeks and again they may continue for a year. Therefore, *the adult performer must spend 30 minutes relaxing, loosening, strengthening, and preparing the joints for running*. This time can be reduced if one uses swimming as his cardiovascular agent.

PHASE I—PREPARATORY EXERCISE, 30 MINUTES
(FOLLOW THE EXACT SEQUENCE)

#61—ARM SWINGING

Swing arms alternately forward and rearward in a full range of motion, *exhale* at full swing. Simultaneously march in place lifting feet 1-2 inches off the floor.

REPETITIONS = 20-25

61

#62—TRUNK TWISTER

Standing, place hands in neck-firm position elbows drawn back. Turn body to left, *exhale*. Repeat to right, *exhale*.

REPETITIONS = 10L, 10R

62

#63—ROCK AND TOUCH

Sit on ground in tuck, roll back extending legs with straight knees, and touch feet to floor, *exhale*.

REPETITIONS = 8

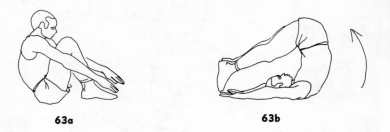

63a

63b

#64—TUCK AND ROLL

Lie on back (supine position). Bring both knees to chest and clasp them with hands, *exhale*. Roll on right side and repeat alternately.

REPETITIONS = 10-15

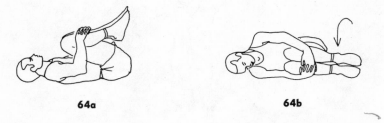

64a

64b

#65—*ROW THE BOAT*

Sitting position, reach forward with back straight and touch toes, *exhale*. Pull arms backward in rowing motion.

REPETITIONS = 10

65a

65b

#66—*SIT ROTATOR*

Sitting position legs extended. Rotate to left swinging left arm sideward, right hand on hip, *exhale*. Repeat to right.

REPETITIONS = 8L, 8R

66a

66b

#67—SIT-TUCK

Sitting tuck position, extend legs to V-sit, inhale, return to tuck and *exhale*.

REPETITIONS = 5-10

67

#68—FOOT ROCKER

Standing, rock back on heels curling feet, *exhale*. Rock forward on outer border of feet to toes, inhale.

REPETITIONS = 10

68a

68b

#69—ABDOMINAL STRETCHER

Lie prone, arms at side shoulder level. Raise chest and arms and simultaneously left leg, inhale. Return to floor, *exhale*. Repeat to right side.

REPETITIONS = 10

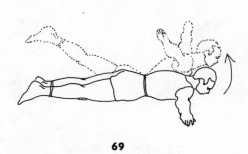

69

#70—ALTERNATE LEG RAISERS

Lie supine, hands palms down under buttocks. Alternately raise legs with straight knees in a scissors fashion to 90° and *exhale*.

REPETITIONS = 25

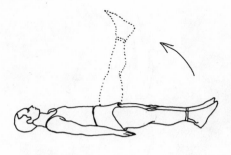

70

#71—BRIDGE ROCKER

Lie on back, feet touching buttocks, hands palms down, fingers pointing towards body. (1) Raise up onto head and feet using hands to absorb part of weight. (2) Roll to right. *Exhale.* (3) Roll to left. *Exhale.* (4) Return to floor.

REPETITIONS = 5

71a   **71b**

#72—BODY HANG

Standing, permit trunk and arms to bend forward and hang in a loose, stretched, and relaxed position for ten seconds (breathe freely). Next, come to an erect body position with arms overhead, stretch upward and inhale deeply. Repeat forward trunk flexion position for 30-60 seconds.

REPETITIONS = 2-4

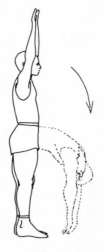

72

#73—INCH WORM

Body flexed at hips with feet flat on floor and hands on floor in front of feet as close as possible. Walk forward on hands in short steps until stretched out to front support, breathe freely. Next, walk forward with the feet in short steps until returning to original position.

REPETITIONS = 5

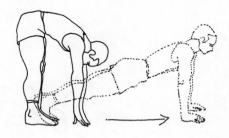

73

#74—SQUAT SWING UP

Standing arms outstretched overhead, lower trunk into squat position, *exhale,* swing arms rhythmically down and rearward followed by knee extension. Bend knees into squat, *exhale,* and bring arms forward and upward overhead as the knees and hips are extended and body returns to original upright position. Inhale during knee extension.

REPETITIONS = 10

74a

74b

74c

#75—ROPE SKIP (OR RUN & HOP)

kip rope single footed with arms extended laterally to permit a omfortable chest position and body mechanics or posture. Use 0-12 foot rope and skip slowly and rhythmically.

EPETITIONS = 120 SKIPS

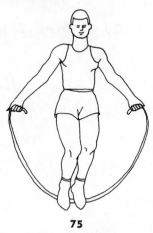

75

#76—FOOT FLEXOR

tanding, rotate feet in circle keeping weight on periphery of foot, lockwise then counterclockwise. Next in stride position force rear eel to floor and stretch achilles and then roll over foot and stretch orsum (instep) of foot. Reverse and stretch opposite achilles and orsum. Repeat foot circles and achilles stretching alternately.

EPETITIONS = 5-10

76a

76b

#77—TEN COUNT PUSH UPS

Front support, (1) dip (2) pushup, *exhale* (3) kick left foot laterally-forward, *exhale,* (4) return to original position (5) kick right foot laterally-forward, *exhale* (6) return to original position (7) lift left leg upward, *exhale* (8) lower leg to floor (9) lift right leg upward, *exhale* (10) return foot to floor.

REPETITIONS = 5-10 (50-100 COUNTS)

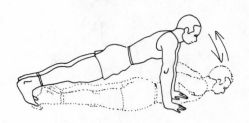

77a

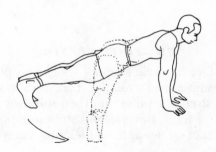

77b

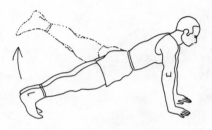

77c

#78—SWINGING ARMS

Standing with elbows flexed and hands at shoulders. Swing right arm upward then outward laterally in a large circle. Repeat to left.

REPETITIONS = 10-15

78

#79—JACK KNIFE SIT UP

Lying supine, arms on flooroverhead. Quickly come to sitting jack knife position on buttocks with hands touching toes, *exhale*. Lower to floor.

REPETITIONS = 10

79

#80—FRONT KICK

Standing arms at side-horizontal. Kick or lift right foot forward
and simultaneously swing both hands forward and touch toe, *exhale*
Return to original position. Repeat with left foot. Perform in rhyth
mic manner.

REPETITIONS = 10L, 10R

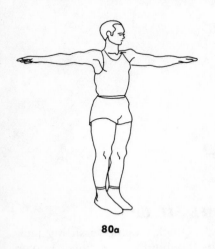

80a

80b

#81—SQUAT STRETCH

Squat position hands on floor palms down outside of knees. Extend
knees and inhale, keeping palms on floor. Return to squat, *exhale*

REPETITIONS = 10

81a

81b

#82—DOUBLE LEG RAISER

Lying supine hands under buttocks palms down, lower back touching floor. Raise both legs with straight knees, *exhale*. Lower legs to floor carefully, inhale.

REPETITIONS = 5-15

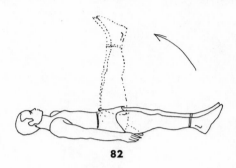

82

#83—TRUNK CIRCLER

Front support, rotate trunk to left and lower to floor, *exhale*. Raise trunk and one-half circle to right, *exhale*.

REPETITIONS = 5-10

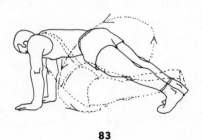

83

#84—FIGURE EIGHT

Lying supine hands under buttocks palms down, lower back touching floor. Lift both feet off floor, knees straight. Circle feet in small arc to left and repeat to right performing a horizontal figure eight. *Exhale* at center of eight and inhale at top of each circle.

REPETITIONS = 5-10

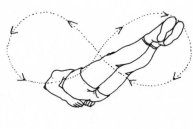

84

#85—BELLY ROCKER

Lying prone arms at sides. Roll to left and then to right, *exhale* center and inhale laterally.

REPETITIONS = 10

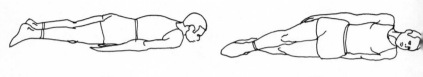

85a   **85b**

#86—TUCK SIT UPS

Lying supine, arms outstretched on floor overhead. Execute a siting tuck, arms and hands clasping shins, *exhale*. Return to floor, nhale.

REPETITIONS = 10-15

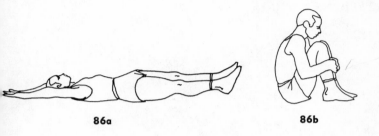

86a

86b

#87—LATERAL FOOT ROCKER

Standing position. Roll weight over to left foot outer border, *exhale*, then roll to right and *exhale*.

REPETITIONS = 5-10 R and L

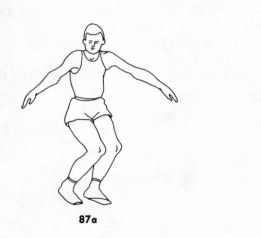

87a

87b

#88—*FULL SWING*

Standing arms outstretched overhead and hands clasped. Swing the trunk and arms right, continue in a full circle by bending forward and continuing to the left and raising to the upright position passing forward in a trunk flexed position, *exhale*. Reverse to left. Perform rhythmically.

REPETITIONS = 10-15

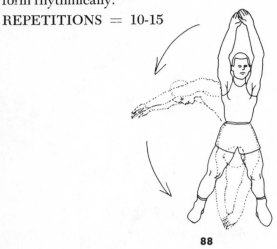

88

#89—*TEN COUNT WRINGER*

Lying supine arms on floor laterally at shoulder level. (1) Kick left foot to right hand, *exhale*. (2) Return to start, inhale. (3) Kick right foot to left hand, *exhale*. (4) Return to start, inhale. (5) Draw both knees to chest. (6) Rotate both knees to right, and touch floor, *exhale*. (7) Return knees to chest, inhale. (8) Rotate knees to left, *exhale*. (9) Return knees to chest, inhale. (10) Return feet to floor, *exhale*.

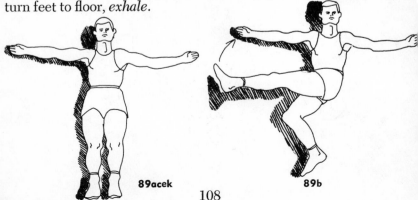

89acek   89b

89d

89fhj

89g

89i

#90—*BACK RESTER*

Lie supine, back flat, knees flexed, toes in and heels out. Rest for
1-2 minutes. Rotate head clockwise and counterclockwise if desired.

90

SUPPLEMENTAL PROGRAMS

Additional programs arranged in proper sequence can be use
for variety and to supplement the exercise found in Phase I o
Stage III. The numbers refer to the original 90 exercises.

Supplement A—1, 2, 4, 5, 10, 63, 64, 13, 37, 67, 18, 19, 53, 78
75, 40, 72, 82, 9, 52, 84, 51, 83, 86, 87, 77, 1, 7
4, 60.

Supplement B—31, 62, 34, 66, 37, 44, 63, 10, 75, 48, 35, 45, 88
25, 50, 51, 53, 78, 52, 9, 84, 21; 19, 28, 55, 56, 16
26, 58, 30.

Supplement C—80, 33, 69, 3, 54, 22, 21, 6, 8, 42, 43, 17, 57, 39
11, 59, 79, 16, 18, 36, 38, 41, 46, 27, 55, 12, 49, 32
90.

PHASE II—CARDIOVASCULAR FITNESS—30 MINUTES (6TH MONTH AND THEREAFTER)

Again the second phase of the 30-30 program is cardiovascula
activity namely, running. It could be swimming, cycling, vigorou
hiking, rope skipping, cross country skiing, rowing, orienteering, o
skating. It may be continuous activity or interval, depending upor
the individual's capacity.

Again we refer to Karvonen (46) and the use of a heart rate dur
ing exercise which is about 70% of the working pulse (see Chapte
5). The performer's pulse should reach about 140-150 per minute
and remain at that level during the sustained portion of the cardio
vascular exercise (about 15 minutes). It should be noted that the
maximum heart rate is reduced as a result of training according to
Montoye (68) by about 14 beats/min. in young men. This drop
would be less in middle-aged men, but it must be considered be
cause the well-conditioned male may attempt to elevate his hear
rate when it actually is already at maximum.

To determine maximum heart rate, use Table 10A in Appendi
A. It is best to start with an assumed maximum Heart Rate of 170
or less. The resting heart rate is obtained by averaging several days
counts prior to arising in the morning.

Several rules should be observed: (1) warm up with 10 minutes
of running by using interval training (run-walk); (2) after warm
up, run continuously for 15-20 minutes; (3) if continuous running

s too vigorous, then use interval running; (4) record immediate ecovery heart rate and get it up to 70% of working rate; (5) cool down by alternating 20 steps of walk and slow run for five minutes and follow with five minutes of flexibility-stretching activity; (6) if you are fatigued one hour after running, your are overdoing. Reduce the workout and use more rest intervals.

RUNNING PROGRAMS

Use several programs for variety and fun. Avoid monotony. Follow all programs with a 5-minute cool-down and 5 minutes of flexibility and stretching.

RUN FOR FUN PROGRAM

Run and walk for 30 minutes as the spirit moves you. Adjust this each day as you see fit.

1, 2, 3 PROGRAM

Run 1', 2', 3', 2', 1' (13') double (26') with 1 minute walking between run intervals, or—run 1, 2, 3, 4, 3, 2, 1 (22') or run 1, 2, 3, 4, 5, 4, 3, 2, 1, (33').

10-10-10 PROGRAM

Run and walk alternately for 10 minutes, then run continuously for 10 minutes at a given pace, i.e., 5-6-7 MPH. Continue another 10 minutes at a faster pace, i.e., 6-7-8 MPH. Cool down for 5 minutes and do 5 minutes of flexibility exercises.

15-MINUTE PROGRAM

Warm up for 7-8 minutes, then run 15 minutes continuously and follow with 4 minutes cool down and 4 minutes of flexibility work.

DISTANCE PROGRAM

Run continuously 2, 3, 4, or 5 miles starting slowly using the distance as part of the warm-up. Be sure to cool down and perform stretching afterward.

440 PROGRAM

Starting slowly, gradually increase the pace while alternately running a 440 and walking a 220 (yards) in between.

880 PROGRAM

Repeat the 440 Program, using 880 and 440 yard distances.

DEVISE YOUR OWN PROGRAM

Arrange a variety of running programs of your own design using a careful 10-minute warm-up, a heart rate of 70% of working rate, and a cool-down-flexibility session at the end.

SPECIAL PROGRAMS

These should be designed by the physician with the help of the exercise leader to fit special cases, i.e., hypertension. Avoid any speed or sprint work in cases of post-infarct, hypertension, and emphysema. Sprint running is to be almost totally avoided in most adults. "Steady-state" or interval running or other cardiovascular exercise is of greater value and little risk.

ENVIRONMENTAL AND OTHER FACTORS IN EXERCISE

HEAT

The use of interval methods with shorter running and longer rest intervals is recommended. Remove all unnecessary clothing. Excessive sweating is to be avoided at *all* times. It has no real place in fitness. Swimming may be substituted for running during hot weather. Ambient temperatures above 80°F may give rise to some difficulty in maintaining body heat regulation, depending upon the relative humidity. Body core temperatures below 105°F for 10-20 minutes in well-conditioned adults presents no problems. However, in obese, poorly acclimated, and untrained subjects, body temperatures of 102-103°F may cause some difficulties and should be guarded against. Several days to a week are needed to acclimatize to hot environments.

DIETING

Low caloric intake may present problems due to low blood glucose and depletion of glycogen (energy) stores in the liver. In such cases when this occurs, followed by exercise, the muscles stop contracting due to glycogen depletion. Victims should be fed sugar or high energy food immediately. They will quickly respond and muscle movement will be resumed. Call a physician nevertheless.

COLD

Adequate clothing is essential for warmth while exercising in cold atmospheric temperatures. Indoor warm-up without undue sweating prior to running outdoors will help the subject. Acclima-

zation is essential and should occur by short exposures over several
ays to several weeks. It is necessary for the air to be warmed prior
entering the lungs.

ILLNESS

One should *not* exercise during an infectious disease. Clearance
y the physician is essential prior to returning to a program of
xercise.

GYMNASIA TEMPERATURE

Ideally a 60° temperature and 40% relative humidity should pre-
ail in the gymnasium. If outdoor temperatures are low, then the
ymnasium temperatures may be below 60°F.

MUSCLE SORENESS

Careful stretching and avoidance of strength and speed work
ill minimize soreness. Running on the whole foot is essential in
reventing calf soreness. Excessive sweating causes a loss of salt
nd vitamin C which should be replenished in the diet, but not to
n excess of salt. Intake twice daily is preferable (17, 69).

EXERCISE AND FITNESS FOR WOMEN

The program of exercise designed herein can be followed by
ost women as readily as by men. Individual differences will vary
idely regardless of sex and must be carefully considered for each
bject.

The 90 prescribed exercises and running programs can be accom-
lished by most women. The two women in the San Diego State
rogram perform at least as well as the average men. Even in the
nning phase they are in the middle of the pack and readily run
e mile in 8 to 9 minutes after a year's training.

Heart rates are about 5 beats above those for men; yet the 70%
ethod of Karvonen (46) is satisfactory and reliable in determin-
g dosage. Obese women will need careful watching just as their
ale counterparts. Hypertension is slightly greater in middle-aged
omen than men, thus about one in five will have high blood
ressure.

Women may have difficulty with ambient heat due in part to a
ck of acclimatization and inability to sweat. Care in exercise
hould be taken. Light clothing and shorter intervals with less
tensity are recommended.

Chapter VII

EXERCISE PRECAUTIONS

An exercise program leader in adult fitness, or any individual participating in a program, must be aware of certain factors that counteract the benefits of exercise. Recognizing these deterrents often makes the difference between a successful or unsuccessful exercise program for an adult. The following is a list and brief discussion of some of the more important negative forces that may interfer with a good exercise program.

SPASMODIC EXERCISE

Spasmodic exercise is probably more detrimental than no exercise at all (22). It prevents the gradual conditioning and slow cardiovascular changes so necessary for fitness adaptation. Three to four times a week are minimal exercise sessions for optimum benefit. The middle-aged exerciser cannot crowd his exercise intervals into one day, for fitness cannot be stored by the body (23). It must be continually replenished.

PROLONGED FATIGUE

Prolonged fatigue after exercise should be avoided. It indicates too vigorous a program if fatigue lasts two hours or more following an exercise session. The body has not yet had time to adapt to that heavy a load of work. The subsequent workouts should be decreased in their intensity to prevent prolonged fatigue. Exercise should leave an individual with a sense of pleasant relaxation, not excessive tiredness.

ALCOHOL

Alcohol and exercise do not mix. Alcohol constricts the coronary vessels of the heart (97) and may cause death due to oxygen insufficiency with vigorous exercise. Several hours (at least four) should elapse between alcohol intake and an exercise session. The better conditioned and trained, the less the risk. But for the adult just beginning his fitness program, alcohol followed by exercise is hazardous.

CIGARETTE SMOKING

Cigarette smoking tends to undo the gains made by exercise 16, 94A). Cigarette smokers never attain the high levels of fitness f the non-smokers. There is probable interference with oxygen xchange across the lung membrane in the smoker. The individual iterested in his fitness should stop smoking.

CHEST PAIN

Any male over 30 years of age who is overweight and underexer-ised is coronary heart disease prone (57, 98). If chest pain de-elops during physical exercise, the exercise should be stopped im-iediately and the person placed at rest. If the pain disappears ith rest, he should be examined and cleared by his physician be-ore restarting the training program.

HEADACHE AND FAINTNESS

Vascular insufficiency of the brain may be manifested by head-che and faintness brought on by exercise and subsiding with rest. 1edical evaluation is again indicated.

SHORTNESS OF BREATH

Obstructive pulmonary disease is found in emphysema, asthma nd bronchial tube spasm from smoking (94A). It is manifested by hortness of breath on exertion. Positive results of an exercise rogram are very slow in these cases and much more time is needed or adaptive changes to occur.

COMPETITION

Competition in fitness programs is undesirable. Individual im-rovement and progress are important, not progress in competition vith the group. Rarely do two or more individuals begin exercising t the same level of fitness. Adult fitness is an individual develop-nent and individual progress is the criterion for success.

SPORTS

A sports program is not a fitness program. Sports are important n American culture and very desirable for the young, but they ave a limited place in most adult fitness programs (50). Most ports are spasmodic and not rhythmic. The game dictates the in-ensity of the activity and frequently creates a sudden overdemand n the heart and vessels. Seldom are recreational sports preceded

by an adequate warm up for vigorous play, so injuries frequentl
result in the adult. Sports such as golf and bowling are of almos
no cardiovascular benefit for they lack sustained activity of the e
durance type.

SWEATING AND SALT

Excessive, purposeful sweating should be avoided. Rubber c
plastic suits that increase sweating are of no value in an exercis
program. Clothing should be light and should allow as much vent
lation as possible. The weight lost by sweating and dehydration
not a permanent loss and is soon regained with fluid replacemen

Most physiologists agree that salt tablets are not needed eve
when exercising during the hot summer months (69). Any sa
lost with perspiration during exercise is better replaced by the libera
use of table salt with meals than by ingesting salt tablets. The tab
lets frequently cause gastrointestinal upsets and other undesirab
effects.

STALENESS

It is possible for an adult to run too much and become stale b
trying to over-achieve in his individual fitness program. This
manifested by excessive fatigue, loss of enthusiasm, and decrease
performance. Occasionally a person may become so enthusiasti
over his fitness that too much emphasis is placed on exercise goal
with decreasing emphasis on his life goals. This, too, eventuall
leads to staleness. The problem is easily solved by decreasing th
frequency or intensity of the exercise sessions for a time. A bette
perspective soon occurs.

MEDICATIONS

Regular exercise occasionally lowers the need for certain medica
tions and dosage adjustment is needed. A good example of this i
that insulin requirements of the exercising diabetic are often de
creased. Drugs used to lower high blood pressure may also nee
adjustment for regular exercise has a beneficial effect on blood pres
sure and less blood pressure medication is needed as fitness im
proves.

OVEREMPHASIS

Although exercise is a very important phase of total fitness, it i
not a panacea for all diseases nor is it one's ticket to eternity. I
should not be emphasized to the exclusion of the other component

of total fitness: correct diet, adequate rest and sleep, emotional stability and maturity, relaxation, correction of any medical problems, and satisfaction in one's daily life.

REMEMBER YOUR AGE

Volleyball, handball and other power games should be avoided during the first three months of adult training. The muscles, joints and ligaments are not ready for sudden explosive movement until they have been conditioned by progressive training.

At first, the running phase of the program should be on soft ground if possible. This helps to prevent the tibial pain (shin splints) that occurs so commonly during early months of training in the adult.

Adults should not do deep knee bends (54), duck-walk exercise and other activities that fully flex the knee joint (squat style activities). Ligament problems, cartilage tears and total loosening of the knee joint are mechanical possibilities with these exercises (54). Half knee bends are permissible and of value if performed with the feet flat.

TIME

Do not hurry fitness. Time is required for both musculoskeletal and cardiovascular adaptation. If the program is hurried, injuries and discouragement may result. Remember, fitness is a *lifetime* dedication.

Chapter VIII

THERAPEUTIC EXERCISE FOR MEDICAL PROBLEMS

There is considerable evidence in the medical literature that therapeutic exercise is of value in specific disease states. It is known that the reserves of the body are lost if one is always at rest. Recovery from surgical procedures and certain medical illnesses are more rapid if activity is allowed early in the convalescent period. The reparative powers of the body are stimulated by movement and tissue atrophy is retarded. These observations have encouraged the return of therapeutic exercise in recent years in certain cardiorespiratory or metabolic diseases. In many areas of the United States exercise programs are used to rehabilitate heart attack, hypertensive, and pulmonary disease patients (40, 73), along with traditional medical therapy.

There must be some modification of the exercise program for these problem cases. In addition there are certain general rules that apply to all medical cases undergoing exercise training. Before reviewing exercise modifications for specific disorders, let us examine the general rules that apply to all exercise program participants with a medical problem.

GENERAL RULES FOR ALL MEDICAL PROBLEMS

1. A medical approval prior to beginning a fitness rehabilitation program must be obtained. Cooperation with the physician is essential and consultation and progress reports to him are important. This is part of the total rehabilitation program teamwork so necessary for successful long-term management.

2. A personal interview to thoroughly explain the exercise program before starting it is important. This interview is to assess motivation and to assure cooperation because irregular, half-hearted attendance will do more harm than good.

3. Laboratory and clinical evaluation should be made before starting the fitness program. In addition to blood pressure, pulse rate, blood count, selected blood chemistry, and pulmonary studies, there should be sub-maximal work capacity tests on a bicycle ergometer, treadmill or bench. These tests should have continual elec-

trocardiographic monitoring all during the stress by a physician skilled in electrocardiogram interpretation. These tests are important for baseline data with which to compare progress. They also indicate many times the degrees of abnormality the subject has at the start of his program.

The sub-maximal work capacity tests with electrocardiogram monitor should be repeated monthly as objective indicators of progress and as guidelines to vary the amount of work done in the program.

If available, telemetering of electrocardiograms during an exercise session at regular intervals is of great value in determining progress.

4. A slow, careful warm up is mandatory. Arm and upper body strength work should be avoided (86, 93). Stretching and flexibility calisthenics in the supine position are always preferable. The intensity or load of the contraction must be light. Limit the repetitions to 6 to 10 per exercise. Accentuate exhale so breath holding does not occur. Alternate the flexibility calisthenics with frequent, short, two to four minute periods of walk-jog.

5 Limit the group to four or five individuals to one instructor for the cardiovascular (running) phase of the program. This provides close supervision and observation of each person during the workout.

6. There should be 2 minutes of continual walking before the running phase of the program is started. This is an additional specific warm-up activity for the cardiovascular system. It also permits adjustment to the upright posture.

7. The running phase of each workout should have slow progression of work intensity. For example, the running phase should begin with a 50 second walk followed by a 10 second jog. This should be repeated several times and then gradually the jogging interval should increase. Toward the end of the session the intervals might have progressed to a 2 or 3 minute jog followed by a 1 minute walk. The important point is the slow, gradual progression.

8. Keep the pulse rate below 140 per minute at all times for the first four months. This a way to prevent undue stress and to control exercise intensity while early adaptation is taking place.

9. Each participant should be taught to take his own pulse rate. He should learn to count his radial, apical or carotid pulsations accurately for 10 seconds then multiply by 6 to obtain a 1 minute estimate. In this way the work intensity can be monitored at all times

by the group leader. Taking one's pulse is easily learned after a few practice sessions.

10. It is of value to keep records of the amount of work done and the pulse recovery after running. This should be done frequently as a monitoring device. As the participants become more fit and better adapted to running the maximal pulse and pulse recovery may be recorded at less frequent intervals.

11. Observe for pallor, excessive sweating, excessive shortness of breath or anterior chest discomfort such as a feeling of heaviness or chest pressure. If any of these signs or symptoms occur, the exercise should be stopped immediately and the subject rested. When full recovery ensues, the workout intensity should be decreased.

12. Testing, monitoring and observing are of particular importance during the first four months of an exercise program. By the end of this period enough adaptation has occurred that the danger has lessened. After four months more latitude can be allowed in the exercising sessions.

13. Three exercise periods per week is minimal. Four times per week is excellent. Under these conditions cardiovascular changes occur optimally. With less than three times per week, the changes are too slow or may not occur at all.

EXERCISE AND CORONARY HEART DISEASE

One year should elapse after a heart attack before starting an exercise program of the type described in this book. A progressive walking program before a year would be desirable if supervised by a physician. A cardiovascular running program, however, is best delayed until a year has passed.

The principles discussed in the general rules apply particularly to the post heart attack participant. Careful supervision, close observation for signs of distress, long, slow warm-up, gradual increase in the running intervals and electrocardiographic monitoring are of prime importance.

In addition fear of exercise is often a problem. Activity has been curtailed for so long that any activity that produces some physical stress may cause anxiety. This decreases with the restoration of confidence in movement. At first, the anxiety itself may cause chest discomfort. Slow, gradual progression of activity is the best antidote for this fear.

Chest pain due to decreased coronary artery blood flow (angina pectoris) may be brought on by exercise. If this does not improve with diminished intensity of exercise, it is sometimes best to discontinue the running program entirely and return to a walking pace. The angina pectoris case often does well on a swimming program. The buoyant effect of the water takes away some of the physical stress of exercise. Occasionally an individual who is unable to walk without anginal chest pain is able to participate in a swimming program and make important cardiovascular adaptive changes. Periodically a return to the land program should be tried.

There is medical evidence that there are two types of coronary heart disease. Both benefit by exercise. The first is the result of diminished size of the coronary vessels that supply the heart and an inadequate number of these vessels to supply the blood and oxygen demands of the heart. This is the classical "hardening of the arteries" of the heart. Those who make exercise a habit develop a better blood supply to the heart muscle by retarding the "hardening" (atherosclerotic) process and by increasing the number of capillaries to supply the heart. The second type of coronary heart disease is the result of the influence of the involuntary nervous system (neurovegetative), and the chemicals produced by nerve excitation, on the heart muscle in sedentary living. The preponderance of sympathetic-adrenergic nervous system tone increases the metabolic vulnerability of the heart muscle (75, 77). It produces oxygen wastage, diminished blood flow and distinct arease of damage to the heart muscle that leads eventually to heart disease. This inactivity-induced neurovegetative imbalance is reversible by appropriate and persistent exercise training.

In the area of Adult Fitness there is no more gratifying experience than to witness the physical and emotional improvement of the heart atack victim in an exercise rehabilitation program.

EXERCISE AND HIGH BLOOD PRESSURE (HYPERTENSION)

Again, the general rules of therapeutic exercise apply.

The most important additional element in the training of hypertensive cases is to extend the training period each session and decrease the exercise intensity. There should be a long warm-up and a long exercise period of slow, steady jogging interspersed with intervals of walking rather than bursts of strenuous activity. Increase the amount of jogging time but decrease the intensity of the running phase. This should be followed by a long cool-down period of alternate slow walk-jog.

The slow, prolonged training leads to a drop in the diastolic pressure causing a widening of the pressure gradient. This results in an increase in blood flow to the muscles and heart. The increased blood flow improves the nutrition of the muscles and removes unneeded residues of burnt muscle fuels (39).

EXERCISE AND LUNG DISEASE

Obstructive lung disease includes such respiratory problems as emphysema, asthma and chronic bronchitis.

Diaphragmatic breathing exercises should be taught but their therapeutic value is of question.

Walking and a slow jog should be stressed, because shortness of breath occurs rapidly with increased work load. The jog should be a little faster than a walk. Again, low intensity work preceded by a long, gradual warm-up is the principle in lung disease cases. High intensity work produces shortness of breath so quickly that no cardiovascular or pulmonary benefits are received. Controlled medical management, particularly of the bronchospastic component, is essential to improve exercise tolerance (65).

EXERCISE AND MUSCULOSKELETAL PROBLEMS

If medical evaluation reveals no fracture, vascular thrombosis, subluxation or other disease states and if the diagnosis of a soft tissue injury has been established, the subject can usually be helped by flexibility-relaxation exercises on an individual basis. There should be no running on an injured part until the acute inflammation has fully subsided. To maintain cardiovascular endurance until healing takes place, it is possible to exercise with the stationary bicycle or by swimming (99, 100).

EXERCISE AND PSYCHOLOGICAL PROBLEMS

There are exercise participants who have a fear of physical activity. There are others who are chronically tardy, or always underachieve by inadequate work, or are irregular in class attendance. Sometimes they develop physical symptoms as a result of their anxiety. These individuals are not poorly motivated, they are anxious and fearful. They require individual counseling and guidance and a better understanding of exercise principles. Their activity pattern should be low gear until confidence is gained. Although their progress and improvement is slow at first, more harm than good is done by trying to increase the work load too rapidly.

Often a participant who seems uncooperative, indifferent or frankly cynical of exercise, is actually anxious and fearful. Constant reassurance and his own gradual progress will eventually change his attitude.

EXERCISE AND OBESITY

Overweight and lack of exercise are often related (20). Those who are overweight tend to exercise less and lack of exercise tends to add weight.

Losing weight depends on the balance between calories expended by activity and calories acquired by ingestion. Other factors ("glandular") are rarely important. As physical energy is expended weight loss will occur. If caloric intake is reduced while additional calories are burned weight loss is assured.

No matter how strenuous the exercise program there are not enough hours in the day to burn off fat if one is overweight and continues to overeat. A fitness program is no license to stuff oneself. The caloric intake for each individual should be determined by his personal physician and may vary from time to time depending on the weight loss progress. Weights should be checked and recorded weekly and the overall pattern reviewed. Optimum weight loss proceeds at approximately two pounds per week as the combined result of both exercise and diet.

FINAL COMMENTS

This chapter has been long, but for a good reason. There is a great challenge in the field of therapeutic exercise in physical disease. Much additional study and work are needed in this area. Most of this chapter is the result of over nine years of observation, trial and error on the part of the authors. We feel that fitness rehabilitation can make important contributions to traditional medical treatment. While physical immortality is unattainable, lean and fit individuals certainly beat the odds.

BIBLIOGRAPHY

1. *A National Program to Conquer Heart Disease, Cancer, and Stroke.* The President's Commission on Heart Disease, Cancer, and Stroke. Vol. 1 Dec. 1964. U. S. Government Printing Office.
2. Armstrong, C., Unpublished M.A. Thesis, San Diego State College, 1965
3. Asmussen, E. & M. Nielsen, Cardiac Output during muscular work, *Phsio Reviews* 35:778, 1955.
4. Astrand, I., Aerobic Work Capacity in Men & Women, *Acta Physio. Scand* 49, Supplement 169: 1-92, 1960.
5. Astrand, P.O., *Experimental Studies of Physical Working Capacity,* Copenhagen, E. Munksgaard, 1952.
6. Astrand, P.O. & I. Rhyming, A Nonogram for Calculation of Aerobic Capacity from PR during Submaximal Work. *J. App. Phys.* 7:218-21, 1954.
7. Astrand, P.O. & Saltin, B., Oxygen Uptake during the first minutes of heavy muscular exercise, *J. App. Physio.* 16:971-976, 1961.
8. Astrand, P.O., T. E. Cuddy, B. Saltin, & J. Stenberg, Cardiac output during submaximal & maximal work, *J. App. Physio.* 19:268-274, March, 1964.
9. Astrand, P.O., Human Physical Fitness with special reference to sex and age, in Jokl, E. & E. Simon, *International Research in Sport & Physical Education,* C. C. Thomas, Springfield, Ill., 1964, pp. 517-559.
10. Astrand, P.O. et al., Intra-arterial blood pressure during exercise with different muscle groups. *J. App. Phys.* 20:253, March 1965.
11. Astrand, P.O., Personal Communique, 1966, San Diego, California.
12. Balke, B., Biodynamics, in *Medical Physics,* ed. by Glasser, Yearbook Publishers, Chicago, 1960, pp. 50-52.
13. Balke, B., The effect of physical exercise on the metabolic potential, a crucial measure of physical fitness, *Exercise & Fitness,* Athletic Institute, Chicago, 1960.
14. Barcroft, H. and Millen, J., The blood flow through muscle during sustained contraction, *J. Physiology* 97:17-31, 1939.
15. Behnke, Albert, The rate and development in change in physique & body composition through physical performances, Paper presented at 14th annual meeting, Amer. College Sports Medicine, Las Vegas, Nevada, 10 March 1967.
16. Bellet, S., Adrenergic effects of nicotine on coronary blood flow & blood lipids, in *Prevention of Ischemic Heart Disease,* edited by W. Raab, C. C. Thomas Publishers, Spring field, Ill., 1966.
17. Bernstein, R., Excretion of Vitamin C in Sweat, *Nature* 140: 684, 1937.
18. Best, C. H. and Taylor, N. B., *The Physiological Basis of Medical Practice,* Wms. & Wilkins, Baltimore, 1961.
19. Booth, R. W. & J. M. Ryan, Clinical use of the valsalva maneuver, *The Heart Bulletin,* 10:111-113, Nov.-Dec. 1961.
20. Bowerman, Wm. J. and W. E. Harris, *Jogging,* Grosset and Dunlap, New York, N.Y. 1967.

21. Braunwald, E., et al., Circulatory response of patients with idiopathic hypertrophic sub-aortic stenosis to nitroglycerin and to valsalva maneuver, *Circulation* 29:422-431, March 1964

22. Burt, J. J., Blyth, C. S., & Rierson, H. A., The effects of exercise on the coagulation fibrinolysis equilibrium, *J. Sports Medicine*, 4:213-216, Dec. 1964.

23. Carlsten, A., The Influence of Age on Active & Non-Active Athletes, Paper given at Congress of Sports Medicine, Pan-American Games, Winnepeg, Manitoba, Canada, July 24, 1967.

24. Carpenter, I. M., *Tables, Factors, and Formulas for Computing Respiratory Exchange and Biological Transformations of Energy*, Washington, D. C., Carnegie Institute, #303C, 1964, 4th Edition.

25. Collins, W. E., Inc., *Clinical Spirometry*, published by W. E. Collins, Inc., Braintree, Mass., 1965.

26. Comroe, J. H., et al., *The Lung*, Yearbook Publishers, Chicago, 1955.

27. Consolazio, C. F., R. E. Johnson & L. J. Pecora, *Physiological Measurements of Metabolic Functions in Man*, McGraw-Hill, New York, 1963.

28. Cooper, J. M. & R. B. Glassow, *Kinesiology*, St. Louis, C. V. Mosby Co., 1963.

29. Cratty, B. J., *Social Dimensions of Physical Activity*, Prentice Hall, Inc. Englewood Cliffs, New Jersey, 1967.

30. Cureton, T. K., et. al., *Physical Fitness Appraisal and Guidance*, C. V. Mosby Co. St. Louis, 1947.

31. Cureton, T K., *Physical Fitness Workbook*, C. V. Mosby Co., St. Louis, 1947.

32. Cureton, T. K., Relationship of physical fitness to athletic performance & sports, *J.A.M.A.* 162:1139, Nov. 17, 1956.

33. Cureton, T. K, *Physical Fitness & Dynamic Health*, Dial Press, New York, 1965

34. Cureton, T.K., Personal Communique.

35. de Vries, H. A., Effects of Exercise upon Residual Neuromuscular Tension, Paper presented to the National Convention of AAHPER, Minneapolis, May, 1963.

36. de Vries, H., *Physiology of Exercise*, Wm. Brown Co., Dubuque, Iowa, 1966.

37. Fox, S. M. & J. S. Skinner, Physical activity and cardiovascular health, *Am. J. Cardiology* 14:731-746, Dec. 1964.

38. Fox, S. M. and J. S. Skinner, Some planning in the United States for further studies to define the relationship between physical activity and coronary heart disease ,*Physical Activity and the Heart*, edited by Karvonen, M. J. & Barry, A. J., C. C. Thomas, Springfield, Illinois, 1967.

39. Guild, Warren R. *How to Keep Fit and Enjoy It.* Cornerstone Library Publications, N.Y., N.Y. June 1967 (Revised Edition).

40. Hellerstein, H. K., A primary and secondary coronary prevention program—In progress report, in Raab, W., *Prevention of Ischemic Heart Disease*, C. C. Thomas, Springfield, Ill., 1966.

41. Hettinger, T. & Muller, E. A., Muskelleistung und Muskeltraining, *Arbeitsphysiologie*, 15:111-126, 1953.

125

42. Horkheimer, M., New Patterns in Social Relations. *International Research in Sport and Physical Education*. Jokl, E. (Ed.). Epringfield, Ill., Charles C. Thomas, 1964.
43. Horvath, S. M., Univ. of California, Institute of Environmental Stress. Techniques in use, 1965.
44. Horwitz, M., The recall of interrupted group tasks: an experimental study of individual motivation in relation to group goals. *Hum. Rel.* 1963,6.
45. Jacob, J. S., Psychiatry, Body Image, and Identity. Address given at AAHPER National Conference, 1962.
46. Karvonen, M., E. Kentala, & O. Mustala, The effects of training on heart rate, *Ann. Med. Exper. Fenn.* 35:307-315, 1957.
47. Karvonen, M. J., Effects of vigorous exercise on the heart. *Work and the Heart.* ed. by Rosenbaum, F. F., & Belknap, E. L., Paul Hoeber N.Y., 1959.
48. Kasch, F. W., A comparison of the exercise tolerance of post-rheumatic & normal boys, *J. Assoc. Phys. & Mental Rehabilitation*, 15:35-40, 1961
49. Kasch, F. W. & W. H. Phillips, Diffusion of CO_2 in meteorological balloons and oiled syringers, *Research Quarterly* 36:104-105, March 1965.
50. Kasch, F. W. et al., Maximum work capacity in middle-aged males by a step test method, *J. Sports Medicine*, 5:198-202, Dec. 1965.
51. Kasch, F. W., W. H. Phillips, W. D. Ross & J. E. L. Carter. A step test for inducing maximal work, *J. Assoc. Phys. — Mental Rehab.* 19:84-96, 1965.
52. Kasch, F. W., et al., A comparison of maximum O_2 uptake by treadmill & step test, *J. App. Phys.* 21:1387-1388, 1966, July.
53. Kasch, F. W., J. E. L. Carter, W. H. Phillips, W. D. Ross & J. L. Boyer, A training program for middle-aged males, *J. Phys & Ment. Rehab.*, 21: 102-104, May-June, 1967.
54. Klein, Karl K., *The Knees*, All-American Productions and Publications, Greeley, Colorado, 1967.
55. Kraus, Hans et al., Minimum muscular fitness tests in school children, *Research Quarterly*, 25, No. 2:178-188, May 1954.
56. Kraus, Hans, Preventive aspects of physical fitness, *New York State Journal of Medicine*, 64, No. 10, May 15, 1964.
57. Kraus, H. & W. Raab, *Hypokinetic Disease*, C. C. Thomas, Springfield, Ill., 1961.
58. La Due, J. S. et al., The Periodical ECG During Exercise, paper at A.M.A. meetings, Miami, Florida, June 1960.
59. Marcus, F. I., et al., Hemodynamic effect of the valsalva maneuver in muscular stenosis, *Amer. Heart J.*, 67:324-333, March 1964.
60. Master, A.M., The ECG & two-step exercise. A test of cardiac function on coronary insufficiency., *Amer. J. Med. Science*, 207:435-450, April 1944.
61. Master A. M., The ECG & two-step exercise. A test of cardiac function on coronary insufficiency., *Amer. J. Med.* Science, 207:435-450, April 1944.
62. Master, A. M., Two step exercise electrocardiogram: test for coronary insufficiency, *Ann. Int. Medicine*, 32:842, May 1950.

63. Masters, A. M. & Rosenfeld, I. Two step exercise test: Current status after 25 years, *Modern Concepts of Cardiovascular Disease*, 36:19-24, Apr. 1967.

64. Mayer, J., Exercise and weight control, Johnson, *Science & Medicine of Exercise & Sports*, Harper, New York, 1960, pp. 301-310.

65. Millman, M., W. Grundon, F. Kasch, B. Wilkerson, & J. Headley, Controlled exercise in asthmatic children, *Annals of Allergy* 23:220-225, May 1965.

66. Mills, H. & A. A. Kattus, Emphysema response to forced straining (valsalva), *Circulation* 17:65, Jan. 1958.

67. Mitchell, J. H. et al., The physiological meaning of the maximum oxygen intake test, *J. Clin. Invest.* 37:538, 1958.

68. Montoye, J. J., Inter-relation of maximum pulse rate during moderate exercise, recovery pulse rate, and post-exercise blood lactate, *Research Quarterly* 24, No. 4, 453-458, Dec. 1953.

69. Morehouse, L. E. & Miller, A. T., *Physiology of Exercise*, C. V. Mosby Co., St. Louis, 1959.

70. Morris, J. N. & M. D. Crawford, Coronary heart disease and physical activity of work, *British Medical J.* 12:1485, 1958.

71. Motley, H. L., The use of pulmonary function tests for disability appraisal, *Diseases of the Chest*, 24:378, Oct. 1953.

72. Mukerji, N. P., An investigation of ability to work in groups in isolation. *Br. J. Psychol.*, 1940.

73. Naughton, J. Cardiopulmonary responses during physical training in patients who have recovered from myocardial infraction, In Raab, W., *Prevention of Ischemic Heart Disease*, C. C. Thomas, Springfield, Ill. 1966.

74. Phillips, W. H. & W. D. Ross, Timing error in determining maximal oxygen uptake, *Research Quarterly* 38:315, May 1967.

75. Raab, W., Neurohormonal atherogenesis, *Amer. J. Cardiology* 1:113, 1958.

76. Raab, W., Civilization induced neurogenic degenerative heart disease, Origin and prevention. *International Research in Sport and Physical Education*. Jokl, E. (Eds.) Springfield, Ill., C. C. Thomas, 1964.

77. Raab, W., The adrenergic-cholenergic control of cardiac metabolism and function, in *Advances in Cardiology*, 1:65, S. Karger, Basel, New York 1956.

78. Raab, W. & H. J. Krzywanek, Cardiac sympathetic tone and stress response related to personality patterns and exercise habits, in *Prevention of Ischemic Heart Disease*, ed. by Raab, W., C. C. Thomas, Springfield, Ill., 1966.

79. Robinson, Sid, Experimental Studies of Physical Fitness in Relation to Age, *Arbeitsphysiologie* 10:251-323, July 1938.

80. Rogers, F. R., The significance of strength tests in revealing physical condition, *Research Quarterly* 5:43-46, Oct. 1934.

81. Rosenblum, R. & A. J. Delman, Valsalva's maneuver and the systolic murmur of hypertrophic subaortic stenosis, *Amer. J. Cardiology*, 15:868-870, June 1965.

82. Rosene, V. J., Unpublished Masters Thesis data, San Diego State College, 1967.

83. Royce, J., Isometric Fatigue Curves in Human Muscle with Normal & Occluded Circulation, *Research Quarterly*, 29:204-212, 1958.
84. Royce, J., Univ. of California, Berkeley, 1964, Personal communique (to F. Kasch).
85. Schaefer, Hans, Social & Preventive Medicine in the Medical Curriculum in *Prevention of Ischemic Heart Disease*, ed. by W. Raab, C. C. Thomas, Springfield, Ill., 1966.
86. Scheuer, J., Myocardial metabolism in cardiac hypoxia, *Am. J. Cardiology*, 19, 385, March 1967.
87. Schnitzer, K., *Electrocardiographic Techniques*, New York, Grune & Stratton, 1960.
88. Scholander, P. F., Analyzer for accurate estimation of respiratory gases in one-half cubic centimeter samples, *J. Biol. Chemistry*, 167:235-250, Jan. 1947.
89. Sharpey-Schafer, E. P., Effects of valsalvas maneuver on normal & failing circulation, *British Med. J.* 1:693-695, March 1955.
90. Simonson, E. & Enzer, N., Physiology of muscular exercise and fatigue in disease, *Medicine* 21:345-419, Dec. 1942.
91. Sjostrand, T., Functional capacity and exercise tolerance in patients, in Gordon, *Clinical Cardiopulmonary Physiology*, Grune & Stratton, New York, 1960, pp. 201-219.
92. Smoldlaka, V., Interval training in heart disease, *J. Sports Medicine*, 3:93, June-Sept. 1963.
93. Stenberg, J., P.O. Astrand, B. Ekblom, J. Royce, & B. Saltin, Hemodynamic response to work with different muscle groups, sitting & supine. *J. App. Phys.* 22:61-70, Jan. 1967.
94. Steinhaus, A. H., *Toward an Understanding of Health & Physical Education*. Wm. Brown, Dubuque, Iowa, 1963.
94A. Surgeon General's Report, The Report of the Advisory Committee, *Smoking and health*, U. S. Dept. of H.E.W., Public Health Service, 1964.
95. Taylor, H. L., Buskirk, E. R., & Henschel, A. Maximum O_2 intake as an objective measure of cardiovascular performance, *J. App. Physio.* 8:73, 1955.
96. Tuttle, W. and S. M. Horvath, Comparison of effects of static and dynamic work on blood pressure and heart rate, *J. App. Physiol.* 10:294-296, 1957.
97. Webb, W. R. & I. U. Degerli, Ethyl alcohol and the cardiovascular system *J.A.M.A.*, 191:1055, Mar. 1965.
98. White, Paul Dudley, The contribution of Exercise to the Prevention of Disease, address given at Pan American Games, Chicago, Sept. 1959.
99. Wilson, I. H. & F. W. Kasch, Medical Aspects of Swimming, *Medical Hydrology*, Vol. 7, Phys. Med. Lib., Licht, New Haven, 1963.
100. Wilson, Ira & F. W. Kasch, Swimming as a clinical tool, *J. Phys. & Mental Rehab.*, 21:82-84, May-June 1967.
101. Zinsser, H. F. & C. F. Kay, The straining procedure as an aid in the anatomic localization of cardiovascular murmurs and sounds, *Circulation*, 1:523-535, Jan-June 1950.

APPENDIX A

TABLE 1A

MASS TESTING FLOOR PLAN

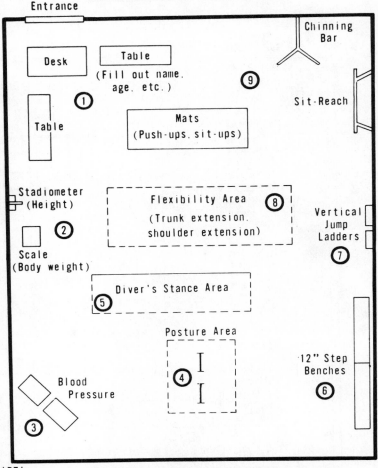

AREA

1—QUESTIONNAIRE
2—HT—WT—GIRTHS
3—BLOOD PRESSURE
4—POSTURE—FEET
5—BALANCE

6—STEP TEST (CV)
7—VERTICAL JP (POWER)
8—FLEXIBILITY
9—MUSCULAR ENDURANCE

TABLE 2A

SAN DIEGO STATE COLLEGE (1966) ADULT PHYSICAL FITNESS—RECORD FORM

I.D. No. _____
Name _____ Age _____ Ht. In _____ Ht. Cm. _____ Wt. Lbs. _____ Wt. Kg. _____ S.A.(M²) _____
Type Subject _____ Program _____ Referral _____ Date _____

AREA	CARDIOVASCULAR ENDURANCE					BP		PULMONARY FUNCTION		FLEXIBILITY			ENDURANCE STRENGTH MUSCULAR			AGILITY POWER		SWIM		BODY WEIGHT	
DATE	STEP TEST PULSE RATE 1', 21'	MILE RUN TIME MIN.	15' Run DISTANCE	Run	Run	SYST.	Diast.	M B C %	V. C. % TIMED	TRUNK FLEXION Inches	TRUNK EXTENSION Inches	SHOULDER EXTENSION Inches	PUSH-UPS No.	SIT-UPS No.	CHINS No.	ROPE SKIPS No. 30"	VERTICAL JUMP In.	DISTANCE	TIME	Wt. Lbs	DESIRED WEIGHT
Normal Mean																					
% Tile Last Test																					

Remarks:

130

TABLE 3A

MEAN RESTING BLOOD PRESSURE AND STANDARD DEVIATION IN APPARENTLY HEALTHY PERSONS, 20 TO 106 YEARS OF AGE

AGE GROUP	MALES		FEMALES	
	SYSTOLIC	DIASTOLIC	SYSTOLIC	DIASTOLIC
20-24	123 ± 13.7*	76 ± 9.9	116 ± 11.8	72 ± 9.7
25-29	125 ± 12.6	78 ± 9.0	117 ± 11.4	74 ± 9.1
30-34	126 ± 13.6	79 ± 9.7	120 ± 14.0	75 ± 10.8
35-39	127 ± 14.2	80 ± 10.4	124 ± 13.9	78 ± 10.0
40-44	129 ± 15.1	81 ± 9.5	127 ± 17.1	80 ± 10.6
45-49	130 ± 16.9	82 ± 10.8	131 ± 19.5	82 ± 11.6
50-54	135 ± 19.2	83 ± 11.3	137 ± 21.3	84 ± 12.4
55-59	138 ± 18.8	84 ± 11.4	139 ± 21.4	84 ± 11.8
60-64	142 ± 21.1	85 ± 12.4	144 ± 22.3	85 ± 13.0
65-69	143 ± 26.0	83 ± 9.9	154 ± 29.0	85 ± 13.8
70-74	145 ± 26.3	82 ± 15.3	159 ± 25.8	85 ± 15.3
75-79	146 ± 21.6	81 ± 12.9	158 ± 26.3	84 ± 13.1
80-84	145 ± 25.6	82 ± 9.9	157 ± 28.0	83 ± 13.1
85-89	145 ± 24.2	79 ± 14.9	154 ± 27.9	82 ± 17.3
90-94	145 ± 23.4	78 ± 12.1	150 ± 23.6	79 ± 12.1
95-106	146 ± 27.5	78 ± 12.7	149 ± 23.5	81 ± 12.5

± INDICATES STANDARD DEVIATION.
From Lasser, R. P. and A. M. Master, *Geriatrics*, 14:345, 1959, with permission.

TABLE 4A

"MEAN BLOOD PRESSURE"

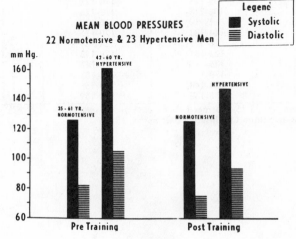

MEAN BLOOD PRESSURES
22 Normotensive & 23 Hypertensive Men

TABLE 5A

WEIGHT TABLES

Weight in Pounds According to Frame
(in Indoor Clothing)

Desirable Weights for Men, Ages 25 and over			
Height (with shoes on) 1-in. heels ft. in.	Small frame	Medium frame	Large frame
5 2	112-120	118-129	126-141
5 3	115-123	121-133	129-144
5 4	118-126	124-136	132-148
5 5	121-129	127-139	135-152
5 6	124-133	130-143	138-158
5 7	128-137	134-147	142-161
5 8	132-141	138-152	147-166
5 9	136-145	142-156	151-170
5 10	140-150	146-160	155-174
5 11	144-154	150-165	159-179
6 0	148-158	154-170	164-184
6 1	152-162	158-175	168-189
6 2	156-167	162-180	173-194
6 3	160-171	167-185	178-199
6 4	164-175	172-190	182-204
Desirable Weights for Women, Ages 25 and over			
Height (with shoes on) 1-in. heels ft. in.	Small frame	Medium frame	Large frame
4 10	92- 98	96-107	104-119
4 11	94-101	98-110	106-119
5 0	96-104	101-113	109-125
5 1	99-107	104-116	112-128
5 2	102-110	107-119	115-131
5 3	105-113	110-122	118-134
5 4	108-116	113-126	121-138
5 5	111-119	116-130	125-142
5 6	114-123	120-135	129-146
5 7	118-127	124-139	133-150
5 8	122-131	128-143	137-154
5 9	126-135	132-147	141-158
5 10	130-140	136-151	145-163
5 11	134-144	140-155	149-168
6 0	138-148	144-159	153-173

For girls between 18 and 25, subtract 1 lb. for each year under 25.
Courtesy of: Metropolitan Life Insurance Company, 1959.

BENEFITS OF RUNNING

(ENERGY EXPENDED)
CALORIES/HOUR WITH EQUILAVENTS – 70 kg MAN

TABLE 6A

PACE
10.5 min mile - 720 cal/hr
9.5 min mile - 800 cal/hr
8.5 min mile - 870 cal/hr

5/8 MILE LAPS
10.5 min mile - 4 $\frac{3}{5}$ / 30 min
9.5 min mile - 5 / 30 min
8.5 min mile - 5 $\frac{3}{5}$ / 30 min

SITTING
100 cal Per Hr.

RUN–WALK
90 cal / 10 min

RUN NON-STOP
290 cal / 20 min

480 cal / day
$$\begin{array}{r} 380 - 30\ min \\ + 100 - 30\ min \\ \hline 480\ cal \end{array}$$
8.5 min mile pace (approx. 3 miles)
30 min calisthenics 100 cal

47000 cal / year
WEIGHT LOSS 12 LBS.

73000 cal / year
WEIGHT LOSS 18 LBS.

10 min.   20 min.

60 min. (30-30)

60 min. SESSION ANNUALLY (2X WEEKLY)

60 min. SESSION ANNUALLY (3X WEEKLY)

133

TABLE 7A

CARDIOVASCULAR FUNCTION
BY 15 MIN. RUN—BALKE (12)

meter/min	VO_2 ml/min/kg	Gradation
	29	VERY POOR
150	37	FAIR (aver.)
200	45	GOOD
250	53	EXCELLENT
300	61	SUPERIOR

Improvement is most important (not gradation)
Change the circulation
S.D.S.C. Program 3 = 171 & 40.4

TABLE 8A

FIFTEEN MINUTE RUN

PREDICTION OF MAXIMUM OXYGEN UPTAKE FROM RUNNING SPEED
from, BALKE, B., *MEDICAL PHYSICS*, 1960, pp. 50-52

Various Classes in Physical Education, San Diego State College, May 1967			
"INDIVIDUAL ADAPTIVES"			
N	MEAN DISTANCE	m/min MEAN RATE	ml/min/kg MEAN PREDICTED VO_2
34	7.522	201.59	45.32
"BOXING CLASSES"			
N	MEAN DISTANCE	MEAN RATE m/min	MEAN PREDICTED VO_2 ml/min/kg
26	8.06	216.0	47.56
"P.E. MAJORS"			
N	MEAN DISTANCE	MEAN RATE m/min	MEAN PREDICTED VO_2 ml/min/kg
15	8.43	227.47	49.49

With the assistance of A. Duke.

TABLE 9A

15 MIN. RUN EQUIVALENTS FOR 440 YD. LAPS AND Vo_2*

440 Yd. Laps	Approx. Vo_2 ml/min/kg	Rate Meters/min	Classifcation (Balke)
5	34	134	
5-1/2	37	148	Fair (150)
6	39	161	
6-1/2	41	174	
7	43	188	
7-1/2	45	201	Good (200)
8	47	214	
8-1/2	50	228	
9	52	241	
9-1/4	53	248	Excellent (250)
9-1/2	54	255	
10	56	268	
10-1/2	58	281	
11	60	295	
11-1/4	61	302	Superior (300)

*Taken in part from Balke, B., *Medical Physics*, 1960, Yearbook Publishers, pp. 50-52.

TABLE 10A

HEART RATE MONITOR
KARVONEN*

MAXIMUM H.R. by AGE (male)		
31-40	41-50	51-60
187 (184-194)	**185** (167-204)	**178** (154-191)

Example:

```
185                        66
-75 resting H.R.          +75
110 working H.R.          141 working H.R.
x 60%                         level during
66.00                         exercise
```

Changes occur above 60%

*KARVONEN. M.J.ETAL., ANN.MED.EXPER.FENN. 35: 307. 1957

TABLE 11A
MEAN C-V* CHANGES IN SEDENTARY MALES
From Physical Training 3 X Weekly

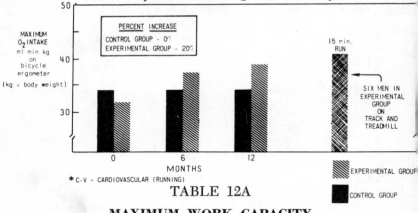

* C-V = CARDIOVASCULAR (RUNNING)

TABLE 12A

MAXIMUM WORK CAPACITY

(Adapted from I. Astrand)*

Age Group Years	Aerobic Work Capacity, Maximum O$_2$ Intake, ml/min/kg**				
	LOW	FAIR	AVERAGE	GOOD	HIGH
Female					
20-29	29	29-34.5	34 5-43	43-48	49
30-39	27	28-33	34-41	42-47	48
40-49	25	26-31	32-40	41-45	46
50-65	21	22-28	29-36	37-41	42
Male					
20-29	38	39-43	44-51	52-56	57
30-39	34	35-39	40-47	48-51	52
40-49	30	31-35	36-43	44-47	48
50-59	25	26-31	32-39	40-43	44
60-69	21	22-26	27-35	36-39	40

*Astrand, Irma, Aerobic Work Capacity in Men and Women with special reference to Age. *Acta Physiologica Scandinavica*, Vol. 49, Supplementum 169, Stockholm, 1960, p. 83.
**Variance in body size is allowed by using kg body weight.

The limiting factor in body work or exercise is the O$_2$ intake. A subject's maximum work capacity is linear to the O$_2$ intake.[2,3] In addition O$_2$ intake is linear to cardiac output.[1] O$_2$ intake then can be substituted for cadiac output. The total body and circulatory efficiency (including the neuro-hormonal controls and compensatory mechanisms) is measured by maximum O$_2$ intake. Only maximum tests measure maximum capacity.[4]

1. Asmussen E. and Nielsen, M., *Physiological Revs.* 35:778, 1955.
2. Astrand, P. O. and Saltin, B., *J. App. Physiol.* 16:971, 1961.
3. Balke, B., Exercise and Fitness, *Athletic Institute*, p. 75, 1960.
4. Bruce, R. A. et al, *Pediatrics Supplement*, 32:753, Oct. 1963.

TABLE 13A

DATA ON WORK CAPACITY

Compiled from ROBINSON, SID, EXPERIMENTAL STUDIES OF PHYSICAL FITNESS IN RELATION TO AGE, *ARBEITSPHYSIOLOGIE* 10:251-323, July, 1938.

Mean Maximal Values (Males)

AGE RANGE	AGE YRS.	N	WT Kg	O² INTAKE* L/min	ml/min/kg	VEN-TIL** L/min	HEART RATE per min	LAC-TATE mg. %	R.Q.	BLOOD SUGAR mg. %	S.A. M²
5.7-6.5	6.1	4	21.0	0.98	46.7	33.3	202	25	0.98	110	0.80
8-12	10.4	9	30.0	1.56	52.1	53.4	211	51	1.12	128	1.06
13-15	14.1	9	55.8	2.63	47.1	92.2	210	62	1.12	138	1.61
16-19	17.4	11	68.5	3.61	52.8	121.0	201	66	1.11	144	1.84
20-29	24.5	11	72.5	3.53	48.7	118.2	197	89	1.21	149	1.91
32-38	35.1	10	79.3	3.42	43.1	122.4	206	97	1.27	133	1.96
41-48	44.3	9	74.1	2.92	39.5	97.6	184	85	1.22	131	1.93
48-57	51.0	7	68.7	2.63	38.4	86.8	185	73	1.17	128	1.83
59-71	63.1	8	67.4	2.35	34.5	80.8	176	58	1.09	123	1.79
73-76	75.0	3	67.4	1.71	25.5	47.7	161	18	0.94	110	1.74

* STPD—All studies done in fasting state (14-16 hours)
** BTPS—The number of subjects changed in some measurements, but the means remained essentially the same.
WORK—Treadmill at 8.6% grade; rate was individualized; duration was 2-5 min., maximal. Warm up was 15 min. on treadmill 8.6%, 4.6 km per hour. A 10 min. rest was followed by the maximal 2-5 min. test.

TABLE 14A
MAXIMUM VO₂ AND HEART RATE WITH AGE AND SEX (MAX. VO₂ IN ML/MIN/KG)

Heading: "MAXIMUM VO$_2$ AND HEART RATE WITH AGE AND SEX (MAX. VO$_2$ IN ML/MIN/KG)"

Source	Age	N	Sex M	Sex F	Max. VO$_2$	Maximum Heart Rate	Type Exercise
Astrand, Irma, *Acta Physio. Scand.* Supp. 169, 49, 1960.	20-29	4	M		52.2	186	Bicycle erg.
	30-39	13	M		39.8 (7.3)	181 (12)	Bicycle erg.
	40-49	9	M		39.2 (5.5)	173 (9)	Bicycle erg.
	50-59	66	M		33.1 (4.9)	161 (11)	Bicycle erg.
Astrand, P. O., *Exper. Studies.* Munksgaard, Copenhagen, 1952.	60-69	8	M		31.4 (5.3)	159 (9)	Bicycle erg.
	20-33	29	M		58.6 (4.5)	195 (11)	Tread & bike
	20-29	8		F	39.9 (4.7)	187 (10)	Bicycle erg.
	30-39	12		F	37.3 (5.2)	185 (7)	Bicycle erg.
	40-49	8		F	32.5 (2.7)	178 (8)	Bicycle erg.
	50-65	16		F	28.4 (2.7)	170 (9)	Bicycle erg.
	20-25	32		F	48.4 (2.8)	199 (10)	Tread & bike
Astrand, P. O., et al., *J. App. Physio.,* 19, 268, 1964.	21-30	12	M		54.0	186 (3.5)	Bicycle erg.
	19-23	11		F	41.4	194 (3.5)	Bicycle erg.
Hollman, W. & Knipping, H. W. *Health & Fitness In Modern World,* Athletic Inst., Chicago, p. 17, 1961.	20-40	80	M		39.6*	176 (8)	Crank or Bicycle erg.
	41-50	36	M		35.7	173 (9)	
	51-60	42	M		29.6	169 (10)	
	61-70	18	M		23.9	164 (7)	
	20-40	127	M		51.3	178 (6)	
Metheny, E. et al, *Am. J. Physio.,* 137, 320, 1942.	19-23	30	M		51.3	194	Treadmill-7MPH
	20-27	17		F	40.9	197	8.6% grade
Robinson, S., *Arbeitsphysiologie,* 10, 251, 1938.	6.1	4	M		46.7	202	Treadmill
	10.4	9	M		52.1	211	Treadmill
	14.1	9	M		47.1	210	Treadmill
	17.4	11	M		52.8	201	Treadmill
	24.5	11	M		48.7	197	Treadmill
	35.1	10	M		43.1	206	Treadmill
	44.3	9	M		39.5	184	Treadmill
	51.0	7	M		38.4	185	Treadmill
	63.1	8	M		34.5	176	Treadmill
	75.0	3	M		25.5	161	Treadmill
Taylor, et al. *J. App. Physio.,* 8, 73-80, 1955.	18.35	30	M		46.9**		Treadmill-7MPH
Dawson, P. & Hellebrandt, F. A., *Am. J. Physio.,* 143, 420, 1945.	53	1	M			180	Bicycle erg.
	71	1	M			148	Bicycle erg.
Dill, D. B., et al. *J. App. Physio.,* 12, 195. 1958.	37	1	M		45.5	172	Treadmill
	66	1	M		35.0	160	
Andersen K. L., *Int. Research Sport & P.E.* (Jokl. & Simmon); C. C. Thomas, Springfield, Ill., pp. 489-500, 1964.	20-30	9		F	36		Bicycle erg.
	17-30	15		F	41		Bicycle erg.
	50-60	6	M		44		Bicycle erg.
	50-60	17	M		36		Bicycle erg.
	50-60	11	M		34		Bicycle erg.
Naughton J., *J.A.M.A.,* 1, No. 11, 103, 1965.	41	10	M		36.1	166	Balke (tread)
Kasch, F. W. et al.***	40-49	18	M		37.3 (5.3)	198 (17.8)	12" step test
	50-59	10	M		39.3 (4.3)	195 (11.1)	

* Calculated from an assumed mean wt. of 75 kg.
** Calculated from an assumed wt. of 75 kg.
*** Difference of VO$_2$ means not significant at .01 level, t = .46, df = 26; difference of heart rate means not signicant at .01 level, t = .46, df = 26.

from—Kasch, F. W., et al, Maximum Work Capacity in Middle-Aged Males by a Step

TABLE 15A

PULMONARY DATA SHEET

NAME _____ DATE _____

AGE _____ HT. (in) _____ (cm) _____ WT. (lb) _____ (kg) _____ S.A. (M²)_____

Temperature of O_2 _____°C Pressure _____mm. Hg.

MAXIMUM BREATHING CAPACITY

1. Record largest 12-second-volume from chart.............#1 _____Liters

2. Multiply #1 by 2 (for 13.5 L spirometer)
   and by 5 (to give total for 1 minute).....................#2 _____Liters/min.

3. Multiply #2 by 11.09 (Gear reduction factor for
   13.52 spirometer)...#3 _____L/min.

4. Convert volume #3 to 37°C saturated, by
   multiplying by the conversion factor. Table
   I, p. 26, spirometer manual or Table
   4.6 _____#4 _____L/min. BTPS

5. Compare predicted and recorded (#4) M.B.C. (BTPS) volumes.

   a. Adults—Formulae: Male $-(97-\frac{1}{2}$ age) x S.A. =_____L/min. % predicted =_____
      (Motley, '50, '52) Female $(86-\frac{1}{2}$age) x S.A. =_____L/min. % predicted =_____

   b. Children (5-18 yrs.)—Predictions from data of Ferris, Whittenberger and Gallagher, ('52) for males; aud Ferris & Smith, ('53') for females.

	Age	Height	Weight	S.A.
Predicted				
% predicted				

Comments _____

_____

TIMED VITAL CAPACITY

1. Record largest total expired volume in 3 second from chart,
   and multiply by 2 (for 13.5 L spirometer)...................#1 _____Liters

2. Record expired volumes in each second and multiply by 2.
   T.V.C. (Raw) 1 sec _____L; 2 sec _____L; 3 sec _____L.

3. Convert volumes in #1 and #2 to 37° saturated, by multiplying by the
   conversion factor. (Table I, p. 26, spirometer manual).
   T.V.C. (BTPS) 1 sec _____L; 2 sec _____L; 3 sec _____L.
                                                        Total_____L (BTPS)

4. Compare predicted and recorded (#3) T.V.C. (BTPS) volumes. (Data from Ferris, et al, '53 for ages 5-18.)

	Age	Height	Weight	S.A.
Predicted				
% predicted				

Comments _____

_____

Extent of tobacco Use _____

TABLE 16A

NOMOGRAM FOR ESTIMATE OF BODY SURFACE AREA

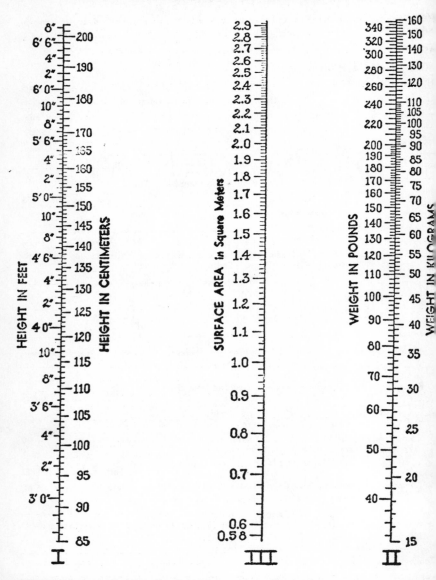

Use height and weight and read center column of bisecting point for surface area.
(From Boothby and Sandiford)

TABLE 17A

SAN DIEGO STATE COLLEGE
ADULT FITNESS

HEALTH EXAMINATION (Required) (To be performed by own physician) Date _____

NAME: _____ Phone _____

       (Last)   (First)   (Initial)

ADDRESS: _____ Age _____

       (Street)   (City)   (Zip Code)

Normal	Abnormal		Please note details of abnormalities below
		Skin	
		Eyes	
		Ears	
		Nose	
		Throat	
		Mouth	
		Teeth	
		Thyroid	
		Heart	
		Lungs	
		Abdomen	
		Hernia	
		Feet	
		Rectal	
		Glandular	
		Reflexes	
		Ch. X-ray	
		Disability	

Laboratory work:

a. Urine, sp.gr. _____ alb. _____ glucose _____ micro. _____

b. Complete blood count: Hbg. _____ Hct. _____ WBC _____ Diff. _____

c. ECG, 12 lead (copy, if available) _____

d. Blood pressure, syst. _____ diast. _____ e. cholesterol _____ mg%

f. other _____

Impression, remarks, recommendations: _____

The above person is capable of participating in a mild exercise under the expert guidance of a competent, well-trained physical educator versed in the physiology of exercise of adults.

       Signed: _____ M.D.

       Type, Name of Physician _____

       Address _____

In case of illness or accident, permission is hereby given to arrange for emergency service:

       Signed: _____

Physician to call _____

       (Name)   (Address)   (Phone)

(*RETURN TO* DR. F. KASCH, MEN'S PHYS. EDUC., SAN DIEGO STATE COLLEGE, SAN DIEGO, CALIF. 92115)

141

INDEX

143